Options Trading Crash Course

The #1 Beginner's Guide to Create Passive Income. Market Evaluation Techniques and the Most Effective Strategies Available Now! Learn How to Trade for a Living

Options Trading Crash Course

The #1 Beginner's Investing Guide to Create Passive Income. Market Evaluation Techniques and the Most Effective Strategies Available Now! Learn How to Trade for a Living

Table of Contents

sources. Please consult a licensed professional before attempting any techniques outlined in this book.

By reading this document, the reader agrees that under no circumstances is the author responsible for any losses, direct or indirect, which are incurred as a result of the use of information contained within this document, including, but not limited to, — errors, omissions, or inaccuracies.

Introduction

I want to thank you and congratulate you for downloading the book, *"Options Trading Crash Course: The #1 Beginner's Investing Guide to Create Passive Income. Market Evaluation Techniques and the Most Effective Strategies Available Now! Learn How to Trade for A Living"*.

Options trading has been doubted for such a long time that a lot of people still think of it as a risky endeavor. So, how can you reduce your risks and maximize your returns? Likewise, how can you improve your knowledge and skills?

This book is going to be your guide in fulfilling all your options trading objectives.

Options are highly popular among economic markets, particularly in the United States. In fact, it is the preferred trading type of the general public, being economically friendly to traders from diverse backgrounds.

Then again, even though a lot of people have already succeeded in options trading, some are still doubtful and hesitant towards it. They do not feel safe and confident that their money will grow.

The truth of the matter is that options trading is good to those who truly understand it. So, if you want to succeed in this endeavor, you have to have a practical trading plan that suits you. You should aim to maximize gains and reduce risks. Your trading plan should be well-structured but simple enough to be followed on a regular basis.

In addition, you need to have the right attitude for trading. Learning about the terms and techniques is great, but developing the right attitude for trading is even better. You need to train yourself so that you can be a smart and disciplined trader.

In this book, you will learn everything you need as a beginner, including terms, strategies, current events related to options trading, as well as the traits that you have to develop if you truly want to succeed.

You will learn about the financial markets and how you can analyze them effectively. You will learn about risks and rewards, and how important practicing is. You will know what paper trading is and why you should do it before you start actual trading.

In addition, you will learn about trading plans, how you can create a good one, and how you can successfully follow it throughout your trading career. You will learn about options and futures, and what their differences and similarities are.

Furthermore, you will learn about the trading platforms that novice and advanced traders use. In the last chapter of this book, you will read about the best trading platforms recommended by experts. You will learn about their features, advantages, and disadvantages. You will also learn how you can effectively choose a trading platform that suits your needs, trading style, and budget.

Indeed, this book has everything you need to know as a beginner options trader. The basics are covered, so you can go from zero to knowledgeable. There are also examples that can help you understand concepts better. Hopefully, you will find this book informative and interesting at the same time.

Thanks again for downloading this book, I hope you enjoy it!

Chapter 1: Introduction to Options Trading

What is trading?

Trading refers to the economic concept that involves the buying and selling of assets, including services and goods. During the transaction, the buyer has to pay the seller his compensation. In some cases, such transactions may also involve an exchange of services and goods between trading parties.

The assets traded in financial markets are called financial instruments, which include stocks, futures, bonds, cryptocurrency, Forex currency pairs, margin products, and options.

What about options trading then?

Well, if you are familiar with stocks and are already comfortable trading them, you will also do well with options.

When it comes to options trading, you have a right to either buy or sell assets at fixed prices prior to their predetermined dates but you are not obligated. Options have values and you should find out more about them.

So, when you buy an option put or call, you are not in any way obligated to sell or buy its underlying instrument. Nonetheless, you have a right to sell or buy at a fixed price. The only risk involved when buying options is related to their price.

Selling imposes an obligation but selling options make you obligated to buy or deliver to the buyer if he exercises the option. When you sell options naked, you may have a risk profile without limits.

However, this may not be ideal for you if you are obligated to do something. Unless you are an advanced trader, you should refrain from selling naked options. You should also have a good strategy for covering downsides.

What should you know about options?

Options are contracts that give buyers a right, but not an obligation, to purchase or sell underlying assets at a certain price on or before a specific date. Just like bonds or stocks, they are securities. They are binding contracts that have strict properties and terms.

Even if you are just a beginner trader who does not know a lot about options, you will be able to understand it better by looking at ordinary day-to-day situations. For instance, if you found a house that you like, you have to have the money to purchase it.

You have to talk to the seller and enter a deal that would benefit you. Negotiate if possible. Say, your money is not enough. You will not have enough money to purchase it for the next three months. You speak with the owner and agree to purchase the house for $200,000 in three months. The owner agrees, yet for this option, you pay $3,000. This scenario would give you two theories:

a. You found out that the house is, in fact, the real birthplace of Albert Einstein. Because of this, its market value goes up to $1M. Since the owner gave you such an option, he becomes obligated to sell the house for $200,000. As a result, you can earn a profit of $797,000.

b. As you tour around the house, you find out that the walls are filled with asbestos and a ghost haunts the bedrooms. Also, you discover a whole family of rats in the basement. Even though you initially thought that you finally found your dream house, you slowly realize that it is the opposite. The house is a disaster! On the bright side, however, since you purchased the option, you no longer become obligated to continue the sale. Then again, you still lose $3,000.

The above-given example shows two focal points: One, if you purchase an option, you gain the right but not the obligation. Two, the option is just a contract that deals with the underlying asset.

So, you may allow the date of expiration to go by and make the option lose its value. Options are also referred to as derivatives. They derive their value from other things. In this example, the underlying asset is the house. Oftentimes, the underlying asset serves as an index or a stock.

Puts and Calls

Puts and calls are types of options. Calls provide the holders a right to purchase assets at a specific price within a certain period of time. Just the same, calls can be compared to long positions on stocks. The buyers of calls usually wish that the stock would substantially increase before the expiration date of the option.

Puts provide the holders a right to sell assets at a specific price within a certain period of time. They are the same as maintaining a short position on stocks. The buyers of puts usually wish that the stock price would go down before the date of expiration.

Options Market Participants

Options markets involve four kinds of participants. These participants depend on the positions that they take. They are the:

a. Buyers of calls
b. Sellers of calls
c. Buyers of puts
d. Sellers of puts

Those who purchase options are known as holders while those who sell options are known as writers. Moreover, sellers tend to have short positions while buyers tend to have long positions.

Take note that sellers and buyers have this vital distinction: the put holders and the call holders are neither obligated to sell nor buy. Instead, they have the option to exert their rights if they want.

Sellers may be required to buy or sell. Selling options is actually more complicated than you may have thought. It can even be much riskier. Thus, you have to learn about the two sides of a contract on options.

The Language or Lingo

In order for you to successfully trade options, you have to learn about the language or lingo involved. There are plenty of terms that traders use when trading. These terms will be discussed later in this book.

The price at which underlying stocks may be sold or bought is known as the strike price. This refers to the price a stock price has to go below for puts or go above for calls before positions can be exercised for profits. This should occur prior to the date of expiration.

Options that are traded on national options exchange are called listed options. You can find examples of these options on the Chicago Board Options Exchange. They have fixed expiration dates and strike prices. Every listed option represents one hundred shares of contract or company stock.

When it comes to call options, the options are claimed to be in-the-money when the share price is beyond the strike price. Put options are in-the-money if the share price is less than the strike price.

Amounts by which options are in-the-money are known as intrinsic values. The overall cost of the option is known as the premium. Such price is based on factors like the strike price, stock price, volatility, and remaining time until expiration. As a beginner, you may not be able to determine the premiums of options right away as this is such a complicated thing to do. As you continue to practice trading, however, you will eventually learn everything about it.

Why Should You Use Options?

Investors generally use options because of two reasons: for speculating and for hedging.

Some people view speculation as betting on security movement. A benefit of options is that it does not limit you to just earning a profit when the market rises. It offers a variety of options, so you can also earn a profit when the market falls or goes sideways.

The territory wherein big money is either made or lost is called speculation. Options use in such manner is the reason why options are said to be risky. When you purchase options, you need to be right in identifying the direction of the movement of the stock as well as the timing and magnitude of this movement.

To achieve success, you have to accurately predict if the stock would rise or fall. You also have to accurately estimate the price change. Your instincts should be reliable enough so that you can know how much money and time you will need for all of this to take place. Do not forget to factor in the commissions. When these factors are combined, you might feel that the odds are up against you.

This sounds tricky; but why do a lot of people still speculate with options. Well, other than versatility, it is all about taking advantage of leverage. If you control a hundred shares with a single contract, it will not take much of a movement in pricing to generate enough profits.

Hedging is another function of options. You can view it as your insurance plan. Houses and cars are not the only ones that have to have an insurance policy. If you want to protect your investments, you have to use options correctly. When used the right way, they would protect you in times of economic downturns.

Those who criticize option claim that if you are not sure about your stock pick and you had to have a hedge, then you should not make any investments. Then again, you can rest assured that hedging strategies are helpful, especially for major institutions.

Even individual investors can find it beneficial. Say, you wished to benefit from the technology stocks as well as their upside, yet you also hoped to limit your losses. You can use options to restrict the downside while still being able to enjoy the full upside. Now, this is cost-effective.

Stock Options

Employee stock options are not available to just about anyone. It is a type of option that can be regarded as a third reason for going with options. A lot of companies use it to attract and keep good employees, particularly the management team.

It is similar to a regular stock option in the sense that its holder has a right yet not an obligation to buy company stocks. However, the contract is between the company and the holder. Normal options, on the other hand, involve contracts between two parties that are not related to the company.

Options in the Real World

Simply learning about the theories on options trading is not enough. You have to put these theories into practice. However, before you set out into the world of trading, it would be wise to learn more from examples.

Let's say, we have a company called Company X. On April 1, its stock price is $67 while its premium is $3.15 for a June 70 Call. This means that its date of expiration is on the third Friday of June while its strike price is $70. The contract's total price now becomes $3.15 x 100 = $315. Then again, in the real world, you also have to consider the commissions. This would give you an amount close to, but not exactly $315.

Keep in mind that stock option contracts are the options to purchase a hundred shares. This is why you have to multiply this contract by one hundred in order to obtain the total price. Thus, a strike price of $70 means that the stock price has to go over $70 before a call option can be worth something. Also, since the contract costs $3.15 for every share, the price of breakeven becomes $73.15.

If the price of the stock is $67, that would be less than the strike price of $70. Hence, the option is useless. Then again, you should remember that you paid $315 for the option. This is why you are down by this much money.

Three weeks after this, the stock price becomes $78. The options contract has gone up together with the stock price. It is now $825. If you subtract the amount that you paid for in your contract, you will earn a profit of $510. This shows you that your money has been doubled. You can sell your options or close your position when you get your profits. You can do this unless the price of stock continues to go up.

Anyway, let's say that the price goes down to $62. Since this is less than the $70 strike price, the option contract becomes useless. So, you go down to $315, which is your original amount. The price swing for the duration of this contract was $825, which would've given you more than double your original investment. Now, you see how leverage works.

Trading Out versus Exercising

You have learned that options are all about having the right to buy or sell the underlying. In reality, however, a lot of options are not exercised.

Going back to our example, you can earn a profit when you exercise or buy or sell the underlying at $70 before selling your stock back at $78 in the market for a profit of $8 per share. You can also retain the stock since you know that you can purchase it at a discounted amount.

Then again, a lot of time holders opt to close out or trade out their positions. The holders choose to sell their options while the writers buy the positions back to close them.

Time Value and Intrinsic Value

Let us learn more about options pricing. Going back to our example, the premium of the option went to $8.25 from $3.15. What happened here is related to time value and intrinsic value.

In essence, the premium of an option is the sum of its time value and intrinsic value. Keep in mind that the intrinsic value refers to the amount-in-the-money. With call options, this means that the stock price is equivalent to the strike price.

The time value represents the probability of the option going up in value. Thus, the option price in our previous example can be said as the premium is equal to the sum of the time value and the intrinsic value. So, $0.25 and $8 combined equals $8.25.

The Options Used by Traders

In general, traders use two types of options: European Options and American Options. American options are exercised any time between the expiration date and purchase date. Our previous example showed this type of option. A lot of exchange-traded options are actually of this type.

On the other hand, European options are exercised only at the end of life. Take note that your geographical location does not have anything to do with the differences between these two types of options.

Long Term and Exotic Options

Long-term investors may prefer holding times of multiple years. These options are referred to as long-term equity anticipation securities. By giving opportunities to manage and control risks, they are basically the same as regular options. Then again, long-term equity anticipation securities provide opportunities for a much longer period of time. Even though they are not available on stocks, these options are still available on many issues.

Exotic Options

Plain vanilla options are known as the simple puts and calls. Although options may be quite hard to understand in the beginning, these simple puts and calls are actually very easy to grasp.

Due to the option versatility, there are a lot of variations and types of options. Those that are not standard are known as exotic options. These are either variations on the plain vanilla payoff profiles or are completely different products that have optionality.

Reading Options Tables

As a trader, the more you learn about the advantages of options, the more encouraged you will be to engage in trading. It is a well-known fact that the trading volume of options has grown over the years. Such a trend has been driven by the introduction of data dissemination and electronic trading as well.

There are traders who use options to make speculations on price direction. There are also those who hedge anticipated or existing positions. In addition, there are those who craft unique positions that provide benefits that are not available routinely to traders of only the underlying stocks, futures, or index contracts.

Regardless of the objectives of these traders, the key to success is to choose the right option or option combination necessary to create a position with the preferred risk to reward tradeoffs. With this being said, the savvy option traders of today are usually searching for more complicated sets of data with regard to options than traders of past years.

Option Price Reporting in the Past

Many years ago, newspapers feature rows of option price data that are quite indecipherable. These data can be found deep within the financial sections. Today, the Wall Street Journal and Investor's Business Daily still have a partial listing of options data for active optionable stocks.

These old newspapers mostly included just the basics such as a C or P to indicate calls and puts. They also included the strike price, open interest figures, and the last trade price. This worked for traders in the past decades. Today, however, option traders know more about the variables that work for options trading. Some of these variables include Greek values that have been derived from option pricing models, implied option volatility, and vital bid or ask spreads.

Because of this, more traders have started to find option data through online sources. Even though every source has its own format for data presentation, the key variables mostly include the following:

a. OpSym – it designates the strike price, the contract year and month, whether it is a put or call option, and the underlying stock symbol.
b. Bid – the bid price is the most recent price offered by the market maker to purchase a specific option. So, if you enter a market order to sell an option, you will be able to see its bid price.
c. Ask – it refers to the most recent price offered by the market maker to sell certain options. So, if you enter a market order to purchase an option, you will be able to purchase it at its ask price.

Keep in mind that selling at the ask and purchasing at the bid is how market makers earn money. It is crucial for options traders to take note of the differences between the ask and bid prices whenever they consider option trades.

In essence, the more active the option is, the tighter the bid or the ask spread. Wide spreads can be a problem for traders, especially those who are short-term. For example, if a bid is $3.40 and an ask is $3.50, you can lose -2.85% on your trade if you buy the option and then sold it later. You will lose this much even if the option price stays the same.

d. Extrinsic Bid/Ask – it refers to how much time premium is built into the price of every option. This is vital to keep in mind because every option loses its premium by the time of expiration. Hence, such value reflects the whole amount of time premium currently built into the option price.

e. Implied Volatility Bid/Ask – it is computed by an option pricing model like the Black – Scholes model. It also represents the expected future volatility level based on the present price of the option as well as other known variables for option pricing. This includes the amount of time until expiration, the risk-free rate of interest, and the difference between the actual stock price and the strike price.

In essence, the higher the implied volatility bid/ask, the more time the premium is built into the option price and vice versa. If you can access the historical range of implied volatility values for security, you will be able to tell if the present extrinsic value level is on the low end or high end. The previous is ideal for buying options while the latter is ideal for writing options.

f. Delta Bid/Ask – Delta refers to the Greek value that has been derived from an option pricing model. It also represents a stock equivalent position for the option. A call option's delta may range from zero to one hundred. The current risk and reward characteristics linked to holding call options with a 50 delta are basically the same as holding fifty stock shares.

In case this stock goes up by one whole point, the option would gain about half a point. In essence, as the delta approaches a hundred, the option trades more and more like an underlying stock. For example, an option with a 100 delta will lose or gain one whole point for every dollar loss or gain in an underlying stock price.

g. Gamma Bid/As – Gamma refers to the Greek value that has been derived from an option pricing model. It also tells you the amount of deltas an option would lose or gain in case the underlying stock goes up by one whole point. For instance, if you purchased March 2010 125 call at $3.50, you will have a 58.20 delta.

In essence, if the IBM stock goes up by one dollar, such option would gain about $0.5820 in value. What's more, in case the stock goes up in price at the present day by one whole point, such option would gain 5.65 deltas as well as would have a 63.85 delta. From here, another point gain the stock price will lead to a price gain for an estimated $0.6385 option.

h. Vega Bid/Ask – Vega refers to the Greek value that signifies the amount by which the option price will be expected to fall or rise based only on a point increase in implied volatility. Hence, if you consider the March 2010 125 call once more, the option price will gain $0.141 if the implied volatility goes up by one point.

This shows you why it is ideal to purchase options when the implied volatility is low. You will pay a much less time premium as well as a rise in the implied volatility will inflate the option price. You will also write the options when the implied volatility is high.

i. Theta Bid/Ask – Keep in mind that options lose the all-time premium by the expiration. Additionally, the time decay accelerates as the expiration date comes nearer. Theta is actually the Greek value that signifies the amount that an option loses with the passage of a day's time.

j. Volume – it merely tells you the number of contracts a certain option has traded during the most recent session. Even though this does not happen all the time, the options that have huge volumes tend to have much tighter bid or ask spreads because there is such a great competition to sell and buy options.

k. Open Interest – it signifies the total number of contracts a certain option has opened but not yet offset.

l. Strike – it refers to the strike price of an option. It is practically the price that the option buyer can buy the underlying security at in case he opts to exercise his option. In addition, it is the price at which the option writer has to sell the underlying security in case the option gets exercised against him.

With regard to puts and options, see to it that you take note of the following:

1. In general, call options become more expensive when their strike price becomes lower. Conversely, put options become more expensive when their strike price becomes higher. With calls, however, the lower strike prices tend to have very high option prices.

   The option prices decline at every higher striker level. This happens because every successive strike price is more out of the money or less in the money. Hence, every one of them has less intrinsic value as compared to the option at the next lower strike price.

   The opposite thing happens with puts. The higher the strike prices go, the more in the money or less out of the money the put options become. This, in turn, results in a more intrinsic value.

2. With call options, the values of delta are positive and are actually higher at a lower strike price. With put options, the values of delta are negative and are actually higher at a higher strike price.

   Such negative values of the put options are derived from the fact that they indicate a stock equivalent position. Purchasing a put option is the same as entering a short stock position. This results in the negative value of the delta.

Option trading as well as the level of sophistication of an average options trader have greatly evolved since this venture started many years ago. The option quote screen of the present time actually reflects these innovations.

It is wise to keep in mind that options trading is not for every person. Not all investors would succeed in this venture. Options can be regarded as complicated trading tools that may be dangerous if you are not educated enough prior to using them. Nevertheless, they can prove to be fruitful if used the correct way.

Basic Pointers to Remember:

- Options are contracts that give buyers a right but not an obligation to either sell or buy an underlying asset at a particular price on or before a specific date.

- Also, options are regarded as derivatives since they derive values from underlying assets.
- Calls give holders a right to purchase assets at a specific price within a certain timeframe.
- Puts give holders a right to sell assets at a specific price within a certain timeframe.
- In essence, there are four kinds of options market participants. These are calls buyers, calls sellers, puts buyers, and puts sellers.
- The buyers are generally called holders while the sellers are frequently called writers.
- Premium refers to the total cost of an option. It is determined by certain factors such as the strike price, the stock price, and the time that remains until the expiration date.
- The price at which underlying stocks may be sold or bought is known as the strike price.
- A contract of a stock option represents one hundred shares of an underlying stock.
- The investors usually use options to hedge and speculate risk.
- The employee stock options are not the same as the listed options since they are actually a contract between the holder

and the company. They also do not involve third parties.

- European and American are the two major classifications of options.
- LEAPS are more commonly referred to as long-term options.

Traits You Need to Develop In Order to Be a Successful Options Trader

Generating income from this venture involves good luck, effort, and attitude.

Patience

Patience is a virtue that can serve you long term. Those who have the capacity to stay calm as they wait are able to reap rewards. In the world of trading, patience is something that you need to have if you want to succeed. After all, good things come to those who wait.

As a beginner, you may find yourself wishing for good luck each time you make a trade. As time goes by, however, you will notice your skills improving. You will begin to develop an intuition. It will become much easier for you to make a decision and trade.

If you still think that patience is not necessary, then ponder this: would a person fly an airplane after just a single training session? Would a doctor perform surgery after reading just one book?

32

Professionals who do well in their career have had years of studying and training. They have gathered enough experience for them to be efficient. You, too, as a trader need the same amount of patience to succeed.

You should refrain from jumping into investments if you are not completely sure about them. You should always think twice, even thrice before making a move. Review your trading plan each time. Think of the possible consequences of your decisions.

For example, if you are just making one percent each week, you should not be disheartened. Do not rush into anything. Instead, you should think of compounding interest. Let your returns accumulate. If you stay patient with trading, your efforts will be rewarded.

Furthermore, you should choose a strategy that allows you to make the most of your time as well as covers your downside. Later in this book, you will be given more information regarding the options trading strategies that you can use.

Nevertheless, no matter which strategy you decide to go for, always keep in mind that patience will bring you to the right opportunity. Do not trade if you are not a hundred percent sure that it is what you have to do. Learn how to wait. Stay patient. Soon enough, you will succeed and acquire wealth.

Perseverance

Successful traders come from different backgrounds and have different trading styles yet they all have a thing in common: perseverance. None of them gave up when things looked bleak. They kept going.

As a trader, it is crucial for you to hold on even when things start to look difficult. Nobody, not even the best trader in the world, can predict what will happen exactly in the future. So, you have to sit tight and keep doing what you are doing in order to achieve your goal.

Once you reach this goal, you should not be complacent and stop. You have to have another goal and keep moving forward. Do not worry if you are not the brightest trader. As long as you have a positive attitude and maintain a desire for learning, you will surely succeed.

A lot of successful traders actually come from humble beginnings. These people were not the most remarkable students. Many others were more intelligent and talented. Nevertheless, they persevered. That's why they were able to attain their trading objectives.

You should create attainable goals and stick to the timeframe. The more you succeed in attaining these goals, the more confidence you build. In turn, you become more experienced and better at making decisions.

Knowledge

You cannot delve into trading blindly. You need to possess the necessary knowledge in order for you to use trading strategies efficiently. Fortunately, there are plenty of tools that you can use. Lots of information are available on the Internet as well as written in books.

You should learn how to create plans for minimizing risks and maximizing profits. You should also learn about entry, exit, and breakeven points. You have to know how to stop losses and generate profits.

Then again, you also have to remember that knowledge is not merely theoretical. It is not enough to simply study trading. Reading books and watching tutorials are helpful, but you also need to gain experience and wisdom.

Smart traders know all about the best strategies. They know when to buy and when to sell. They are aware of the latest trends on the market. However, they also know how to manage themselves, including their emotions.

Remember that emotions are a natural part of being human. There will be times when you will feel emotional towards your options. You might feel scared, happy, or sad with trading. This is why you have to learn how to work around your emotions instead of ignoring or giving in to them. You have to be objective at all times.

Being in the right state of mind is crucial. Use your experiences to your advantage. Each time you trade, see to it that you find the lesson that comes with it. So, next time you find yourself in a similar situation, you will know what to do.

Honesty and Accountability

Every decision you make is your responsibility. This is why you need to be careful with every step you take. You roll the dice. So, you have to live with the consequences.

Pre-Planning

Every trade you make should be pre-planned. This means that you have to be aware of your maximum reward and risk as well as your breakeven points. In addition, you should plan both your entry and exit points whether you want to gain profits or stop losses.

For example, you may base your stop loss on the underlying stock, which is generally more liquid than the options. Hence, it is much easier to make a decision based on stock, future, and other underlying asset prices.

When pre-planning, you should study your chart pattern. This way, you can create your trading plan. You need to be disciplined enough to stick to your plans. Pre-plan before trading and use your experience to do better each time. You can also seek guidance and inspiration from other people's trading experiences. Learn from their mistakes and follow their successful moves.

Resist the urge to change your plan, even though you have had a last-minute idea that you think might benefit you. Always aim to be methodical. Remember that discipline is key to becoming a successful trader.

If you do not know how to manage your finances wisely, no trading system will work for you, not even the best ones. When you stick to good principles on managing money, you will be able to minimize your losses and maximize your gains.

What's more, you will be able to avoid risk profiles that are suicidal. Be wary of unhelpful risk profile curves. Always study these curves so that you can achieve success at options trading.

Chapter 2: Trading Strategies

In order for you to survive the intense competition in the financial markets, you need to use successful and properly tested trading strategies. Keep in mind that if you use a trading style that is based on chaotic cross-betting, you will surely fail. You need to have systematic trading.

The Importance of Using Good Trading Strategies

Systematic trading is vital for long-term success. When you stick to a strategy that lets you stay focus in spite of the huge inflow of economic data and news, you will be able to remain rational. Your analysis process will not be negatively affected by these factors.

In addition, profound knowledge is necessary for the pricing characteristics of certain asset classes or assets. Aside from profound knowledge, you also need technical analysis to set the exit and entry points. Beginner traders tend to fail due to the lack of these analyses.

Take note that you may still profit from merely using a predetermined strategy based on price action. You can measure and improve your own performance. Be careful not to trade chaotically. You should always have a good trading plan so that you can evaluate your performance and have a constant basis for comparison.

When you use a trading system for a long time, you can create a statistical database that would allow you to evaluate its performance. Once you are done with the evaluation, you can start to improve it. Do not forget to change the necessary parameters and compare the new results with your historical data. This would allow you to find out if the upgrade is a success.

Another reason why trading strategies are important is that they help you regulate your emotions. It is natural for humans to be emotional because it is part of their nature. So, when it comes to putting your money at stake, you might become emotional at certain times. After all, you work hard to earn your money. You certainly do not want to lose it.

A lot of traders have a problem with controlling their emotions. They tend to be overcome by greed, fear, and sometimes anger. Do not be like these traders. You should always be calm and collected. Winning and losing come with trading.

There are days when you would lose and there are days when you would win. Even the best traders have experienced defeat at some point in their lives. Thus, you should not be carried away by your emotions when you win and especially when you lose.

Do not allow greed to overcome you when you win. Otherwise, you will start to bet too much than you need to. Do not allow fear to overcome you when you have experienced losses. Remember that the best traders are courageous. They do not avoid entering good positions because they know that they can gain huge profits.

Do not allow anger to overcome you when you do not get the outcome that you expected. Nobody can make exact predictions about the future. Nevertheless, you can make intelligent guesses and study your strategies carefully. A good trading strategy can help you disregard any volatility in your performance. This, in turn, can help you manage your emotions well and concentrate on achieving success.

Furthermore, you should be careful not to overtrade. It is important for you to have a trading system with well-defined exit and entry rules. Otherwise, you can slip into a position opening frenzy. You may overtrade and hurt your chances at achieving success. Always watch your actions. Do not make trades more than you can actually handle.

Selecting the Trading Strategies for You

Every trader is unique. So, you should not expect one trader's strategy to work for everyone else. Different traders follow different strategies as well as make different analyses. There is not a single strategy that works for all. The financial markets continue to change. Thus, you need to grow, change, and evolve with them.

It is wise to study different strategies in order to find out which ones work well for you. Here are some of the trading strategy characteristics that you have to keep in mind:

a. Profitable and effective strategies are simple.

   Professional traders use advanced techniques to increase their chances of success. However, using more techniques than necessary can also be harmful to your success rate. Complex trading strategies can be difficult to use and earn money from. This is especially true if you are a beginner trader without much trading experience.

b. Every strategy needs sufficient testing prior to employment.

You need demo accounts to survive in trading. Traders have to use them, regardless of their experience. After all, these are great for testing new ideas free of charge. Do not forget that various assets have various trading specifications. Hence, you need to study the different strategies carefully.

Remember that a certain strategy may work well for a certain type of investment but not for another. So, a strategy that works great with stocks may not work well with cryptocurrencies. You need to use a demo account to find out about things like this.

c. The strategies used in trading can become obsolete.

Nothing lasts forever, including trading strategies. Those that are effective now may no longer be effective in the future. After all, the development pace of the financial markets continues to evolve. The performance of a trading strategy is expected to diminish at some point. This requires monitoring. When the trading strategy starts to underperform, you can either abandon or fine-tune it.

d. Every strategy is subject to drawdowns.

Take note that even the most successful trading strategies can fail at some point. So, if the strategy that you are using has a 60% success rate, it is possible for your binary option to end up as "out of money". Since losing positions is unavoidable, all you can do is accept losses and follow your trading plan.

Combining Trading Strategies

In order for profits to be gained, trading strategy diversification is necessary. Expert traders do not rely on a single strategy because they know market conditions are diverse. Hence, they need to use a variety of trading strategies to succeed.

Using more than one trading strategy allows you to easily digest the inevitable losses that one strategy can cause. Once these losses start to diminish your confidence, it would be difficult for you to perform at your best. However, once you are able to reap profits, your morale will be improved.

Also, as the financial markets evolve, some strategies start to die down. They are no longer able to keep up with the latest trends. They start to lose their relevance. This is why you should always be prepared to switch to an alternative strategy. Remember that trying to mend a previous strategy can actually do more harm than good. For instance, it may cause you to lose more money in the long run.

Furthermore, asset diversification is a vital hedge against drawdowns. If certain asset classes or assets defy your expectations, specifically after you bought options with a longer maturity, having positions that are opened in other asset classes or assets can offset such losses and keep you at or beyond breakeven.

Then again, since different assets and asset classes tend to have different trading specifics, you have to use different optimized trading strategies. This, of course, calls for a system of strategies used for trading.

Different Options Trading Strategies

The following are some of the strategies that you can use for options trading:

Covered Call

If you wish to buy a naked call option, you need to use buy-write, also known as covered call. This strategy is highly popular amongst traders due to its ability to reduce the risk involved in staying long on stocks while generating income. However, you may have to sell your shares at a short strike price, which is a set price.

Covered call is actually a strategy used by investors who feel that their underlying position is quite bullish in the near term although good for medium to long term. In order for you to be able to use this strategy successfully, you have to buy an underlying stock while simultaneously writing or selling a call option on such shares.

You have to sell a call option on one of your stocks so that you can have a premium inflow. When the underlying increases, so does the profit. However, this profit is capped once it reaches the strike price.

Also, if such underlying crosses this strike price, the payoff will get capped because the call option will incur losses. Nevertheless, you can still generate good income using this strategy if the market is neutral.

What does this mean exactly?

Say, an investor uses a call option on a particular stock that represents one hundred shares of stocks per call option. When this investor buys shares of stock, he has to sell a call option simultaneously. In essence, every one hundred shares of stocks require one call option.

This example illustrates the covered call. If ever the stock price increases, the long stock position covers the short call. As an investor, you may go for this strategy if you have a short-term position in stock as well as a neutral opinion. You may be protected against a decline in the value of the underlying stock or earn an income from the call premium sale.

With the covered call strategy, both your risks and rewards are limited.

Buy Call

This strategy is ideal if you are bullish on the direction of the market going up short term. Also known as Going Long on a Call, Buying Call is the easiest way to make a profit if you think that the market will go up. It is also the most commonly used strategy by beginners.

When you go long on a call option, you can enjoy gains if the underlying stock or index rallies. Then again, if this stock or index makes a correction, you can have risks.

In essence, this strategy comes with unlimited rewards and risks that are limited to your paid premium.

Buy Put

The buy put, also known as go long on a put, occurs when investors become bearish on the direction of the market going down in the short term.

The put option allows the put buyer to sell a stock at a pre-determined price in order to limit his risks. With this strategy, you can be at an advantage if the underlying stock or index goes down. Nevertheless, there are limited risks on the upside when the underlying stock or index rallies.

Sell Call

The sell call, also known as go short on a call, occurs when investors are not bullish on the market. With this strategy, you can gain a premium from the call buyer.

There is limited profit potential in this position. There is also a possibility for huge losses on large advances in the underlying prices. Even though this strategy is fairly simple, it is still risky because the call seller becomes exposed to unlimited risk.

Sell Put

The sell put, also known as go short on a put, occurs when investors are bullish on the direction of the market and they expect the prices of stocks to increase or remain sideways at a minimum.

If you sell a put, you can earn a premium from the put buyer. When the underlying price goes higher than the strike price, the position of the short put allows the seller to earn a profit depending on the premium amount. However, if the price goes lower than the strike price, particularly if such price goes lower than the premium amount, the seller of the put loses money.

Married Put

With this strategy, you can buy assets while simultaneously buying put options for the same number of shares. The put option holder can sell stocks at the strike price. As an investor, you can use this strategy to protect your downside risk as you hold a stock. It works the same way as an insurance policy since it establishes the price floor in case the price of the stock goes down.

Let's say, you buy a hundred shares of stocks as well as a put option. The married put strategy may appeal to you since you get to be protected against the downside in case a negative change occurs in the stock price. Likewise, you can take part in upside opportunities in case the value of the stock increases.

Then again, in the event that the stock does not decrease in value, you lose the amount that you paid in premium for the put option.

Bull Call Spread

With this strategy, you can buy calls at a certain strike price simultaneously while selling the same amount of calls at a higher price. These two call options would have the same underlying asset and date of expiration.

You can use this vertical spread strategy when you are bullish on an underlying asset and you expect a slight increase in asset price. If you use the bull call spread, you can limit your upside on a trade as you reduce your net premium spent.

You can use this strategy if you are moderately bullish on the direction of the market going up in the short term. It actually occurs when an in-the-money call option is bought and an out-of-the-money call option is sold. These two call options should have a similar month of expiration and underlying security.

This strategy's net effect is to pull down the cost as well as breakeven on a long call or buy call. As an investor, you can benefit from this strategy if your underlying stock or index rallies. Then again, you can have limited risk if a correction is made on the underlying stock or index.

Bull Put Spread

This strategy should be used if you are moderately bullish on the direction of the market going up in the short term. It occurs when an out-of-the-money put option is bought and an in-the-money-put-option is sold. These two options should have a similar month of expiration and underlying security. The idea is to buy a lower strike put in order to protect or provide insurance to the put sold.

Bear Call Spread

This strategy is ideal if you are moderately bearish on the direction of the market as well as expecting the underlying to go down in the short term. It occurs when an out-of-the-money call option is bought and an in-the-money call option is sold.

These call options should have a similar month of expiration and underlying security. As an investor, you will receive a net credit since the purchased call has a higher strike price than the sold call.

Bear Put Spread

This vertical spread strategy is preferable if you simultaneously buy put options at a certain strike price while you sell the same amount of puts at a lower price. These options will have the same underlying asset and date of expiration as well.

You can also use this strategy if you have a bearish sentiment with regards to the underlying asset as well as when you expect the price of this asset to decrease. You can expect limited gains and limited losses from the bear put spread.

This strategy should be used if you are moderately bearish on the direction of the market as well as expecting the underlying to go down in the short term. It occurs when an in-the-money put option is bought and an out-of-the-money put option is sold.

These put options should have a similar month of expiration and underlying security. As an investor, you have to pay a net premium since the purchased put has a higher strike price than the sold put.

Protective Collar

When you use this strategy, you have to buy an out-of-the-money put option while you write an out-of-the-money call option. Also, you have to ensure that both the date of expiration and the underlying asset is the same.

You can use the protective collar strategy after experiencing substantial gains from a long position in a stock. It will give you downside protection since the long put locks in the possible sale price. Then again, you may be obliged to sell your shares at a higher price. Hence, you may not be able to gain additional profits.

Say, an investor goes long on a hundred shares of Company X at $50. Supposedly, Company X increases in value to $100 by January. You may sell a Company X March 105 call and buy a Company X March 95 put to gain a protective collar. Remember that until the date of expiration is reached, the trader gets protected below $95. As for the trade-off, you may be obligated to sell your shares at $105 if Company X trades at such a rate before the date of expiration.

Long Straddle

If you simultaneously buy a call and put option on a similar underlying asset with a similar strike price as well as the date of expiration, the long straddle occurs. You may use this strategy if you think that the price of an underlying asset might significantly move out of a certain range yet you are not sure of which direction such a move would take.

In theory, the long straddle allows investors to have a chance at unlimited gains. Likewise, these investors may suffer from a maximum loss that is nevertheless limited to the cost of the two options contractors combined.

Long Strangle

If you buy a put option and a call option that is out-of-the-money on a similar underlying asset with a similar date of expiration, this strategy will occur. With a long strangle, the investor believes that the price of the underlying asset would have a huge movement yet he is not sure about the direction that the move would take.

Long Call Butterfly Spread

With this strategy, you get to combine the bear spread and the bull spread strategies. You also have to use three various strike prices. Plus, every option is for the same expiration date and underlying asset.

You may actually construct a long butterfly spread when you buy an in-the-money call option for a low strike price. At the same time, you can sell two at-the-money call options as well as buy an out-of-the money call option.

The wing widths of a balanced butterfly spread are the same. When you attain a call fly, you can expect a net debit as result. You will then go into a long butterfly call spread if you believe that the stock would not move a lot prior to the expiration date.

Iron Condor

With this strategy, you can hold a bear call spread and a bull put spread simultaneously. It is basically constructed when you sell an out-of-the money put and buy an out-of-the-money put with a lower strike.

The expiration date as well as the underlying asset for every option are the same. The call and put sides also have a similar spread width. If you use this strategy, you can earn a net premium. In fact, a lot of traders rely on it to attain a high probability of generating a small premium amount.

Iron Butterfly

With this strategy, you buy out-of-the-money put and sell at-the-money put. You also buy out-of-the-money call and sell at-the-money call. Every option is on a similar underlying asset and has a similar expiration date. Even though the iron butterfly is quite similar to the butterfly spread, it actually uses both puts and calls whereas the butterfly spread only uses one of the two.

The iron butterfly also combines purchasing protective wings and selling at-the-money straddle. Profits and losses are limited to a certain range. This strategy may work well for you if you typically aim for high income and small gains with non-volatile stocks.

Buy Straddle

The buy straddle, also known as the long straddle, is a non-directional strategy. It is typically used when the investor expects the underlying to show big movements in any direction.

It also involves purchasing a put-and-call on a similar underlying for a similar strike price and maturity. Through this strategy, you can choose to move in either plummeting or soaring direction, giving you a great advantage.

You can earn a profit if there is volatility in the underlying to cover the trade costs. Your loss is also limited to how much premium you had paid when you bought the options. As an investor, all you have to do is to find out if the underlying exponentially breaks out in either direction.

Sell Straddle

The sell straddle, also known as the short straddle, is actually the opposite of the buy straddle. This strategy is used when investors expect the underlying not to show any big movements. Instead, they expect the underlying to show some downside or upside volatility.

With this strategy, a call and a put are sold on the same underlying for a similar strike price and maturity. It also gives you a net income. In the event that the underlying doesn't move in either direction, you get to retain the premium since the call and the put will not be exercised. Then again, if the underlying moves down or up, you may be at risk of unlimited losses.

Long Synthetic

This strategy can be used if you are bullish on the direction of the market. It involves selling put options and buying call options at a similar strike price. These options, however, should have a similar month of expiration and security.

You can say that using the long synthetic strategy is akin to being long on an underlying security. If you go long for this strategy, you can expect to see payoff traits that are the same as holding a features contract or stock. It also has the advantage of being less expensive than purchasing an underlying outright.

Short Synthetic

This strategy can be used if you are bearish on the direction of the market and you expect it to go down soon. This strategy also involves purchasing put options and selling call options at a similar strike price. These two options should have a similar month of expiration and underlying security.

You can expect this strategy to behave exactly like being short on an underlying security. You can also use this strategy when you expect the payoff traits to be the same as being short on a future contract or stock. As for the rewards and risks, you can expect them to be unlimited.

Call Backspread

It is ideal to be used if you are bullish on the direction and volatility of the market. It can be effective if you are both bearish and bullish on the market with a bias to the upside. It involves buying two Out of the Money Call Option lots and selling one In the Money Call Option. These call options should have a similar expiration month and underlying security.

Chapter 3: Advantages and Disadvantages of Options Trading

There are many advantages and disadvantages to options trading that you have to learn about if you wish to be successful in this venture.

The Advantages of Options Trading

Cost Efficiency

With options, you get to enjoy lots of leveraging power. You may actually have an options position that is equivalent to a stock position at a lower margin.

Stock trading requires a higher upfront financial commitment than options trading. The cost of purchasing an option, which includes both the trading commission and the premium, is much less than the cost of purchasing shares.

High Returns

You get to have a better chance at yielding high returns with options trading than with using cash to buy shares. If you are able to choose the correct strike, you can gain an equal profit from the option as you would when you buy stocks. Hence, you can enjoy higher returns since you get to acquire options at a lower margin.

Low Risks

While it is true that options are riskier than equities, they are still more widely used for hedging positions. Take note that the risks involved with options are predefined since the maximum losses may be the premiums paid to purchase such options.

Strategy Availability

There are many different trading strategies that you can use to buy and sell options. Even better, these strategies may be combined to give you more flexibility as well as allow you to develop a strategic position.

Limited Downsides

If you buy a call or put option, you are not obligated in any way to follow through on a trade. In case your predictions on the direction and timeframe of the stock's trajectory goes wrong, you do not get to suffer huge losses. Instead, your losses are merely limited to the amount you paid for the trading fees and contract. Then again, the same thing cannot be said for those who sell options.

More Flexibility

With options trading, you can enjoy more flexibility. After all, before your contract expires, you can execute several strategies that include buying shares and exercising an option to add to your portfolio, selling shares and options, and selling in the money options contracts.

Fix Stock Prices

You can freeze a stock price at a strike price or a particular amount for a certain period of time. This will guarantee that you will be able to sell or buy such stock at such strike price at any time prior to the expiration date of the contract.

The Disadvantages of Options Trading

Less Liquidity

Certain stock options can be highly difficult to trade due to their low liquidity.

High Commissions

Compared to stock or future trading, options trading is more expensive. Then again, there are still discount brokers who can let you trade at a lower commission. Nevertheless, the majority of the full-service brokers charge high fees for options trading.

Time Decay

When time decay occurs, your options premium's value decreases. It continues to decrease each day regardless of the underlying movement.

Non-Availability

Stocks that have been registered with exchanges don't have any options contracts. Because of this, traders often experience difficulty in hedging their positions with their strategies.

Chapter 4: Analyzing the Market

When it comes to stock trading, it is imperative for you to study the market. You need to find out if it has a momentum that can be sustained. You also have to determine whether or not you need to use sentiment analysis and breadth tools.

Keep in mind that the market can be quite unpredictable. The advances on the market also tend to be better when more stocks advance. You can use the options market as a reference when determining the status of the stock market. You can monitor options to determine whether the stocks are advancing or declining.

Pointers to Remember

Before you focus on the market, you may want to learn about interest rates and global economic trends first.

In general, falling or low-interest rates are considered to be bullish for stocks while rising or high-interest rates are negative. Take note that interest rate trends may affect the prices of underlying stocks. This, in turn, can affect the prices of options.

With this being said, it is only sensible to watch for global interest rates. All the markets in the world are linked together, so you have to understand how they move. According to experts, there would be a market inflection point someday. This would cause the stock prices to decline, making stocks unattractive investments.

As for global economic trends, you have to realize that the global economy was generally synchronized until the United Kingdom exited from the European Union and Donald Trump was elected as the United States president. These events have majorly affected the trends in the market.

Identifying Movement Strengths

Every decline and advance on the market is unique. For instance, a moderate advance may occur with a lot of sectors going up together in frenzy. It may also go up with certain sectors and stocks outperforming the others.

If this happens, you should not waste your time trying to figure out what the market would do at any time. You should, instead, focus on analyzing the chances of trend direction continuing. As an investor, you want to trade in the direction of the currently dominant trend on the market.

You may find it quite difficult to have a new position if you think that you have missed a move. Nonetheless, you can still look at the breadth of the market so that you can decide with more certainty if the advance conditions are improving or not. You will also be able to predict downsides better in case the market appears to deteriorate.

Do not forget to use various tools for confirming market assessments. You should also use strategies that would allow you to stay consistent with these assessments. Keep in mind that gaining profits and being successful in trading requires patience, vigilance, and smart use of trading strategies. Whenever you see a possible change in trend, make sure to create a plan as soon as possible so that you can follow the new trend accordingly.

The Market Breadth

The breadth of the market is the heartbeat of the market. It is the one that offers an in-depth look at the market's internal components, which make it rise or fall. If you observe how much stocks advance and decline for a particular index, you will be able to predict the health of its move.

When it comes to markets that rise, you should observe if the gains are spread out amongst major companies. When it comes to markets that decline, you should observe if the bear gets exhausted due to too much participation.

The indicators of breadth include the following:

a. Volume and number for declining and advancing issues
b. The up and the down volumes
c. Number of issues that reach new lows or new highs
d. Issues that trade below or above moving average lines

You can say that an advancing market is bearish if its declining stocks outnumber the advancing stocks in both volume and number. When this happens, the stocks may do well even if the overall market is unhealthy. We call this the bearish divergence.

Conversely, market advances with stocks from various sectors that trade above the moving average is bullish and suggest a healthy increase.

You can use the advance-decline, also commonly referred to as A-D line and Adv-Dec, line breadth indicator. There is no need for you to search for a certain bearish or bullish number. You can simply use it as a tool for diverging or confirming.

The most vital aspect of this breadth indicator is its line because it tells whether the direction of the market is going sideways, up, or down. You can construct this line by maintaining a regular cumulative total of: advance-decline line = number of advancing issues – number of declining issues.

Take note that an index can rise even if the advance-decline line goes down. This can occur when a small number of stocks advance yet the value of the gains from the advancing stocks is higher than that of the losses from the decliners. It can also occur if the component stocks that have a lot of influence on the index increase despite the decrease of most of the component stocks.

If you wish to calculate the advance-decline line as a ratio instead of a cumulative value, remember that the ratio becomes greater than one if there are more advancers and that the ratio moves between one and zero if there are more decliners.

Do not forget to monitor the divergent movements, movements into extreme ranges for possible turns, and the center line's oscillator crosses. The indicators of the advance-decline line may be calculated on any ETF or index that offers regular declining and advancing statistics.

Whenever you monitor the advance-decline line, see to it that you search for advancers that would outpace the decliners in markets that rise as well as declines that would outpace the advancers in markets that fall. This would confirm the index changes. Also, whenever the indicator diverges from the index action, the present trend can be problematic.

As for analyzing such indicators, it would be in your best interest to keep track of their long-term record or history. Consider their twenty-day moving average, the rate of change indicator, and the relative strength index indicator among others. You can stay up to date with the trend once you understand the tops and bottoms of the market. In general, the more information you have, the more successful you can become.

Analyzing the Market Psychologically

It is great to be able to assess the market based on actual facts. However, aside from looking at the physical aspect of the market, should you also analyze it from a psychological perspective?

Well, some people believe that in order for you to be able to understand the market better, you have to know why it does what it does. But are these people correct?

Essentially, it is actually much better to focus on staying on the right side of the trend rather than trying to comprehend why the market does what it does. After all, the market acts on whatever data it receives.

It gives a response based on this data, regardless of whether it is wrong or right. Such response comes from the opinion of the majority. The market basically goes in the direction of the money flow.

Then again, this does not mean that the movement of the market is predictable. People are naturally drawn to fulfilling their self-interest and preserving themselves. Since selling and buying securities means losing or making money, you need to understand that the participants are typically influenced by their own desires. They can be irrational.

Hence, you should learn about the different ways on how you can monitor the conditions of the market as well as the behavior of the crowd. This would allow you to better understand the reasons behind the actions of the market. You can use market sentiment analysis, which can help you determine the human emotion that drives the reaction of the market.

What is sentiment?

Sentiment generally refers to the market's overriding bias. This can either mean bearish or bullish. The human emotion fear coupled with greed can result in a bullish market while fear can be associated with the market's decline.

Regardless of the changes in the economy, greed and fear will surely occur. They will continue the pattern for as long as possible.

You can imagine the market as a very wavy ocean. The undulation of these waves is the sentiments. The waves will continue to show up. However, they can show up in variations. The same thing goes with the market. It would be fueled by greed and fear over and over again. Nevertheless, it would have variations with regard to the period of time in which such emotions rule the underlying dynamics.

Options and stock statistics can be used as sentiment tools. These would give you the data you need about crowd activities in times of declines and advances. You can search for such information on charting packages and exchange websites.

When using sentiment analysis, see to it that you determine the times when fear has become exhausted or when greed is no longer sustainable. At a certain point in time, a major change can happen and you need to be prepared for it. This way, you will be able to quickly respond to the change in direction.

Keep in mind that trading is actually a balancing act. So, you have to focus on the market sentiment. Always remember that whatever happens in the market may not be the same as what you expect. So, you should always be prepared.

Measuring the Actions of Investors

Most of those who use sentiment analysis become doubtful of the trade because it tries to measure bearish and bullish actions as opposed to what is being said about the market or its direction.

As a trader, you need to be mindful of the following factors:

a. A bullish commentary that is contradicted by an unusually high put volume
b. An economic report that yields an enormous swing in the market
c. A huge change in the Federal Reserve's interest rate policy that results in an unexpected reaction
d. Whether or not the traders are bullish or buying calls and selling puts
e. Whether or not the traders are bearish or buying puts and selling calls

The data obtained from options trading usually makes traders doubtful and fearful. Volume and historical volatility let them know how emotions affected previous decisions. Implied volatility, on the other hand, let them know what they can anticipate for the future.

Watching Put and Call Activities

Traders and other investors are mostly optimistic. They often think of the market as bullish. Fortunately enough, the market has a tendency to go up than down. This shows that the trends on the market are generally reflected by the positive disposition of traders and investors.

Keep in mind that observing the bullishness of the market is advantageous. This is because the call volume typically exceeds the put volume, which in turn reflects the market's tendency to advance. It gives you an option activity baseline.

What happens when people get nervous? The put volume goes up.

When you observe the relationship between puts and calls, you will be able to see the extreme levels that correspond with the market reversals. Put volume, whether alone or along with call volume, can be used to measure the complacency or fear that people have towards the market.

The Put-to-Call Ratio

The put-to-call ratio is derived by dividing the volume of the put contract by the volume of the call contract. Its creator, Martin Zweig, predicted that the stock market would crash in 1987. He was able to make this accurate prediction by using such ratio. Today, there are various ratios that you can use to guide you in trading.

The put-to-call ratio focuses on bearish and bullish actions by considering the different participants on the market. Be mindful of the contrarian measures as well. When people become overly bearish, the conditions become right for an upside reversal. When people become exuberant on prospects, the chances of having a decline become higher.

In essence, you can interpret the put-to-call ratio according to the following:

a. Very high readings are considered to be bullish
b. Very low readings are considered to be bearish

How about some good news? You can count on the following for information regarding the readings and indicator construction:

a. CBOE equity P:C ratio
b. CBOE index only P:C ratio
c. ISE Sentiment Index
d. ISE Index and ETF put/call ratio

How can you maximize the sentiment tools available?

First, you have to have knowledge of basic indicator construction information. Next, you have to understand the implications and historical extremes of this tool. Finally, you have to recognize the changes in the market as well as the impact on the indicator data.

See to it that you also get the data from every exchange that performs options trading for the underlying in case you want to zero in on sentiment for individual security. Note that indicators can also exhibit different behaviors during bear and bull markets, as well as during various bear or bull market stages. If you want to use a new indicator, do not forget to verify its performance with the use of a new indicator.

Chapter 5: Fundamental and Technical Sector Analysis

A market that functions properly involves broad advances such as stocks and sectors. At times when broad averages strongly go up, stocks and sectors follow. In a downtrend, the reverse is also true. Stocks, indexes, and sectors usually fall during such times.

Then again, there are always exceptions. In some instances, the market's general trend is not followed by certain sectors. This happens when economic conditions are favorable towards a particular group for a particular timeframe. As the conditions change, however, the sectors that display weaknesses or strengths also change.

When you focus on weak and strong sectors, you are able to customize your trading strategies according to the conditions of the market. Just make sure that you are able to find these sectors. You can use technical analysis such as those geared towards determining relative weaknesses and strengths.

Chart Analysis

Chart analysis focuses on the visual cues that determine volume and price information, which may lead you towards useful market trends. There are actually a variety of data displays and charts that you can choose from. All of these can provide you with a long list of analysis tools. Just make sure that you go for the one that fits your needs best.

Chart Fundamentals

Charts are also commonly referred to as price charts. They are essentially visual price activity records or pictures that are formed from price data plotting. They allow users to see their trading activities over time. Some of the charts that you may encounter are:

a. Line Chart

They are charts that document the movements of prices versus time. A line is used to connect the price data point for every period. These charts also plot the most significant value for the week, day, or any period of time. In essence, they plot the closing price value.

As a trader, you will not have a hard time interpreting line charts since they are fairly easy to understand. You will be able to see the data you need for the trends and price movements when you filter out the noise from the minor movements.

However, even though line charts seem to be great, they also come with certain disadvantages. For example, they do not give any information on day trading strength as well as on price gaps.

Price gaps are made when trading for a period is totally below or above trading for a previous period. This occurs when the market is closed and there is news that affects the company.

b. Open High Low Close Bar Chart

This chart shows the price versus the time. The trading range of the period is shown using a vertical line. The opening prices are shown using a horizontal tab on the left side of the range bar while the closing prices are shown using a horizontal tab on the right side of the range bar.

Every bar is constructed using four price points. The open high low close bar chart is also regarded as more useful over different timeframes since it provides data on both the price gaps and the strength of the trading period.

c. Candlestick Chart

This is perhaps the most popular chart amongst professional traders. It shows the price versus the time and is quite similar to the open high low close bar chart in the sense that the price range between the close and the open for the period is highlighted with a thick bar.

The candlestick chart also shows the gaps and ranges of prices. It also has unique patterns that can help improve your daily analysis. It also has distinct pattern interpretations that describe the differences between bears and bulls. Ideally, you should apply this to your daily chart.

Time Horizon Adjustment

Before you focus on a certain chart interval, it would be best to consider your trading or investment horizon. You have to determine your timeframe and objective for trading options.

You can use technical analysis to help you with your timeframe. In general, long-term trends are stronger than short-term trends. Whenever you look for trends, you should analyze the charts carefully so that you can effectively depict the price action over several time intervals.

The daily chart is generally the chart default. You can use it to plot the price action daily. You can also use a chart that measures minutes, years, weeks, and months. Furthermore, when you complete a market analysis to find good sectors, see to it that you evaluate the following:

a. Long term trends with the use of monthly charts on sectors and indexes
b. Intermediate-term minor and major trends with the use of weekly charts on sectors and indexes
c. Short term minor trends with the use of daily charts

When you recognize the intermediate and major trends first, you will be less likely to make irrational decisions. You will not get caught up in the emotions related to short-term moves.

You can draw a horizontal support line after the price goes down twice for the price level. This line will be confirmed if the third touch of such price level finally holds as well as if the buying demand goes back to the security and makes the price go up.

Supply and Demand Visualization

Surely, you are familiar with the supply and demand on the market. You can count on a chart to display this data. In essence, purchasing demand makes prices go up. The supply creates a selling pressure that makes prices go down. In addition, the volume shows the magnitude of either the supply or demand.

The market does not simply move up or down. The variations in its price are a result of dynamic and constant battles between the bears and the bulls. In this case, the bears are the supply while the bulls are the demand.

There can be a horizontal resistance line and the price can go up to reach a price level two times. This line will be confirmed once the third touch of this price level is able to hold and the selling demand goes back to the security; thus, making the price go down.

Resistance and Support Areas

The resistance and support of the price can stop the current trend. Support is actually a chart area in which buyers go into a trend that falls. It represents the transition from the declining prices, which are driven by the supply to the climbing prices whenever a renewed demand starts at such price level.

On the other hand, resistance is a chart area in which sellers go into a trend that rises. It represents the transition from the climbing prices that are driven by a strong demand to the declining prices whenever a pressure starts at such price level.

Each time you trade, make sure that you observe these transitions. They tend to line up and create sideways trading channels whenever the price moves between them. Just like with every price trend, the longer a price functions as a resistance or a support, the stronger it becomes.

Resistance and support levels are not merely chart points. They are actually areas that you can use when you need to act. For instance, resistance and support levels are helpful in determining the trading positions at exit and entry points.

You can also use them during price projections to determine the profit-taking and the stop-loss exits as well as the calculating risk-reward ratios. More often than not, the price areas that formerly functioned as support function as resistance areas in the future and vice versa. Every time the prices go above the resistance or go below the support, a new price trend tends to occur.

Analyzing Trends

As a trader, you surely know about upward and downward trends. With upward trends, the prices go up and down in a way that rising lines can be drawn under the pullbacks that show higher lows. Upward trends also have higher highs.

With downward trends, the prices tend to fall and retrace in a way that declining lines can be drawn over the retracement peaks, which show the lower highs. Downward trends also have lower lows.

Chapter 6: Risks and Rewards

Risk is a natural part of life. Nobody, not even the so-called psychics, can see the future. So, you can expect trading to be risky as well. Options trading is actually a very risky endeavor. No matter how hard you research and study the market, you still cannot be 100% certain of the outcome. If you are not careful with your actions, you can lose a lot of money.

Experienced traders are generally adept at making decisions regarding their exit position. Before opening a trade, they either go to the exit position through a profit objective achievement or a stop loss. If you want to be a successful trader, you should not merely be good at making decisions. You should also be good at executing your strategies and creating trading plans.

Take note that whether you manually execute your exit or you use an advanced automated order design, there is a tendency for the stocks to gap down below your expected exit level; thus, making you incur much bigger losses. These stocks can be open for trading at a closing price that is way below the previous one.

What's more, if you want to have a manual exit, your position may suffer a much greater hit. The mechanical trading increase by means of preconceived algorithms has caused trading to be more challenging for traders.

In other words, a stock trade's maximum risk can be an entire initial investment. You may lose more money if you use a margin. If you want to avoid such huge losses, you must understand that you can incur major losses. You have to be aware of the reasons why you may end up this way. With enough knowledge, you can reduce your chances of losing a great deal of money.

The Risks of Trading

With risks, there comes rewards. This is the good thing about trading. You can expose yourself to great losses, but you can also expose yourself to great gains. Then again, you have to play the cards wisely. With options trading, risks and rewards can be lopsided. You may find risk-reward profiles to be different even though they seem to be similar at face value.

In fact, when presented with two different trades, you can have more risks in a single trade as compared to the other. This is even if both of these trades have the same reward potential. However, the final outcome would depend on the risk characteristics of your traded security.

Before you start trading, see to it that you fully understand the risk involved. Here are some pointers to keep in mind:

 a. Probability of sustaining a loss
 b. Maximum amount of possible loss

If you wish to be a professional trader, you need to spend enough time learning about possible risks. You have to prioritize this more than knowing about possible rewards. More importantly, you have to learn how you can manage your risks by creating strategies that can limit or decrease your risks while maximizing your profits.

There are two main types of risk: lack of gains and potential for losses. When investments are not able to keep up with inflation or the increasing costs of living, they may be reduced or depleted.

Risking Funds with Stocks

The moment you became a trader was the moment you exposed yourself to risks. Involving yourself in options trading means potentially losing all your investments, regardless of how careful you become.

Take note that there are a couple of ways on how you can establish a long stock position. You can buy the stock on margin with even just 50% percent cash or you can buy the stock with 100% cash.

Even if you may limit how much margin is used to a number below 50%, this ½ of the amount is still the maximum amount that you can use for an initial position. As you know, the prices on the market continue to fluctuate. Thus, when you purchase a particular stock at a particular price, this price can go up, down, or sideways.

Perhaps, the worst thing that can happen is when the price falls and the losses add up. Also, even if the stock price goes up and down, you may still buy-in on a bad day when your particular stock begins on a prolonged downward trend. What's more, if this particular stock stops trading for any reason, you may no longer be able to exit at any level.

Although you may also exit a trade at a certain point, the stock may also go downward to zero. In turn, this would result in a total loss of investment. Thus, your maximum risk when purchasing a stock becomes:

Number of Shares x Stock Price = Risk

The margin has both pluses and minuses. It is also not recommended by most experts. When you buy a stock on a margin, you get to have leverage. This allows you to have more stock for an initial investment. However, this also magnifies your losses and gains.

Say, you bought a particular stock on margin instead of using 100% cash. This doubles your risk by one divided by the initial cash percentage. This is your leverage.

If you want to compute for the maximum risk of purchasing a stock on margin, you may begin by multiplying your initial investment by one divided by the initial margin percentage. After that, you may add the cost of using the margin or the margin interest rate for the holding period of the stock.

When you use a margin to buy a stock, your maximum risk becomes:

Risk = (Number of Shares x Stock Price) x (1 / Initial Cash %)

Make sure that you add the margin interest to your equation. It is computed based on how much money you wish to borrow to purchase the stock. Say, you wish to borrow $10,000 with a 5% margin interest. You can then borrow $500 when you borrow the money for one year. Interest is usually calculated based on 360 days, which is equivalent to one year. So, if you borrow the money for twenty days, you have to divide $500 by twenty. You will then get $25 and your margin cost will be $25.

How about shorting a stock?

Those who do this usually hope that the price of the stock will go down. So, they reverse the order of the stock transaction. Instead of purchasing first and then selling, they sell first and then purchase the stock.

If you wish to sell a stock that is not yours, you have to borrow shares. However, these shares may not be available for selling short if the conditions of the market are not right. Hence, you must always check the short sale list or your broker or directly communicate with them to find out if you can go on with the transaction depending on share availability. Traders who have brokers with active trading accounts usually have smooth transactions.

You may also use the Internet for short selling. When you become an online broker, you can indicate your trading type in the drop-down menu. Your trade will push through when there are available shares for short selling. However, if there aren't any shares, the trade will not push through. You will be given a notification.

When you do brokerage account paperwork, you may provide authorization to lend out the shares in your account, which will then be available to the short-sellers. You may only hold short stock positions in margin accounts.

Take note that stock short selling cannot be done in retirement accounts like the Individual Retirement Arrangement (IRA). Credits may be received for stock sales. However, there may still be margin issues. So, you have to ensure that you truly know about the process before you make any trades.

What about your risks? Shorting a stock can put you in a highly risky position because there's no limit to how high stocks can go upwards. Shorting stocks basically involves unlimited risks.

On the other hand, long stocks represent limited yet high-risk positions. They are limited because stocks may only go down to zero. They cannot go down further. Because of this, the risks stay high. They increase when the margin is used and you are put in a situation in which you may lose more money than your initial investment.

Option Risks, Call Options and Put Options

When you buy both put and call options, you become exposed to risks that are limited to your initial investment. When you sell options, you expose yourself to more risks and greater losses than your initial investment. Such initial investment may differ in size. Nevertheless, whether you buy or sell options, this initial investment is still less than the required investment for controlling the same amount of underlying stock shares.

In dollars, the risk is quite smaller. However, it is vital to recognize that the odds of the purchased options going to zero is very high due to their limited life security. Once the option expires, its value becomes zero unless it is in-the-money.

Call options give buyers rights to buy underlying stocks at the strike price of the contract by its date of expiration. As this expiration nears, the call option loses time value; thus, resulting in losses when the stock trades above the option strike price.

Let's say the stock's price level stays the same. When there is time decay, you can gain losses as a trader. These losses, however, are limited since the option retains its intrinsic value.

When the stock trades below the strike price, the value of the option is all time value. Let's say the stock's price level stays the same. The time value would diminish when you get closer to the expiration date. There can also be a total initial investment loss when this manner continues.

More often than not, stocks fluctuate. You cannot expect them to stand still. So, even though there is a likelihood for the underlying stock to rise in value as it goes above the call strike price, it can still decline in value as well as go below the strike price. When this happens, you may lose all your investments as the expiration date approaches.

With regard to put options, they give the buyer rights to sell underlying stocks at the strike price of the contract by its date of expiration. These options lose their time value as the date of expiration approaches. This, in turn, typically results in losses for the traders when the stocks trade above the option strike price.

When you trade below the strike price, your losses are limited due to the options retaining the intrinsic value. Then again, when stocks trade above the strike price, the value of the option becomes the all-time value. Let's say that the stock stays at the same price level, the time value decreases when the expiration date approaches.

Going on in this manner would lead to a complete loss of the initial investment. Since the price of the stock has a possibility to either fall or rise, there is a likelihood that the underlying stock would rise in value going above the put strike price. When this happens, you may also lose all your investment when the expiration date approaches.

Reaping Rewards

You already know the risks, so why should you still bother to make trades? For starters, investments can beat inflation. Traditional savings may become unreliable. After all, even though their interest rates go up, the rate of return is still going to be likely below the inflation rate.

Hence, if you plan to use the money for more than a sport, you have to assume the risk of trading. If you are willing to take on higher risks, you have to expect rewards that are much better than the money at market rate. Both options and stocks actually give such potential.

Stock Benefits

When you become a stockholder, you may benefit from the gains and dividends of the stock. These gains tend to increase whenever the profits or sales of the company increase as well as whenever there are new technologies or products introduced among other reasons. You can also benefit from the approaches that let you download moves in these stocks.

Chapter 7: Practice, Practice, Practice!

It is imperative for beginner traders to practice. You have to test the water before you dive deeply into it.

Have you ever wondered why professional athletes are so good at what they do? It is because they devote countless hours into practice. They dedicate years of their life into mastering the sports that they are in.

So, even though nothing is truly perfect, there is some truth to the saying that practice makes perfect. Repetition is the key to rewire your brain. When you do something repeatedly, you get used to it.

The same principle works in trading. When you practice using strategies, you get better at them. As a beginner, you can start with paper trading. It is a form of practice trading in which you do not have to use actual money.

Before you shell out any money, you have to try out strategies and do some practice runs. You need to be adequately prepared before you trade in real terms. Likewise, before you use a new trading strategy, you have to understand the rewards and risks of security. You have to practice the trading strategies that you plan to use and you have to thoroughly analyze trades before you execute them.

As a trader, you have to start with paper trading and then transition into active trading through learning and analysis. In essence, you have to move from using concepts into taking actions.

How can you do this exactly?

First, you have to monitor the different components of option pricing as well as paper trading. You have to simulate the live conditions and begin rewiring your brain. You have to do this so that you can get used to dealing with real-time situations. This would give you better intuitions as well as prevent you from making expensive mistakes.

When you develop your skills in backtesting, you implement the best methods and allow yourself to remain in the game long enough to acquire valuable experience. You will eventually reach strategy mastery through experience and practice.

Monitor Option Greek Changes

It is important for you to recognize the right options pricing in strategies. However, it may be more important for you to understand the basic options strategies since they can help you learn more quickly. As a beginner, you have to know how to monitor Greek and price changes under various conditions.

Track Premium Measures

Once you develop your skills with options strategies, you will understand how options premiums get affected by changes in the expiration time and the underlying price.

You have to be active. An ideal way to have a better intuitive feel for the effects from these factors is by tracking the changes in the various components of options prices on a daily basis. You need to gain access to the market prices as well as have a spreadsheet program and an options calculator.

Once you monitor several different options, you will be able to learn about the effects of changing conditions on prices. When you include Greeks in this process, you will be able to understand the factors that play vital roles at various times.

As much as possible, you have to aim to review the tracking prices and markets when the prices move around. This would help emphasize the effects of theta, delta, and gamma on the prices. Make sure that you also learn about Rho, which refers to the measure of influence on interest rates, and Vega, which refers to the measure of volatility.

In addition, before you shell out dollars, see to it that you use a spreadsheet to keep track of the underlying stock price, the in-the-money prices, and the out-of-the-money and at-the-money puts and calls with different expiration dates. You should also keep track of the option intrinsic value, theta, gamma, delta, and options time value.

When you keep track of these values, you will be able to determine the measures that have major effects on options strategies.

Prices of Options and Volatility

The prices of options can be affected by volatility. This can actually be quite difficult to handle because implied volatility is an expression of the expected volatility of options in the future.

Traders, especially beginners, often get confused with the terminologies related to volatility. So, here is a great way to remember things: Past or Historical Volatility refers to the measure of the actual price movement of the underlying stock. Future or Implied Volatility refers to the measure of the price movement of the underlying stock and is derived from the prices of options.

Having a Volatility Grip

A stock's historical volatility can effectively predict implied or future volatility in the same price of the stock in the future. In addition, a primary factor in a stock's actual volatility is the way the options price affects it.

Implied Volatility

It refers to the volatility in the price of stock implied by the price of the option. Since it is also a critical factor in pricing options, it is ideal to study it to the best of your abilities. You see, in terms of implied volatility and trading, you have to remember that high readings can accurately predict major future price movements. Low readings, on the other hand, can accurately predict minor future price movements.

Likewise, when low implied volatility periods are combined with event timing and technical analysis, they can offer good entry points while extended high volatility periods can offer good exit points.

Basically, a 30% volatility for a stock that costs $100 can give you a chance to trade between $70 and $130 in the coming year. The price movement is actually dependent on one standard deviation of the price of a stock, which is typically distributed at 68.2%.

Consider the rules as your guidelines so that you can be guided accordingly. Knowing these rules by heart will allow you to apply them to your trading strategies with ease. You will be able to trade options or stocks naturally.

Say, when you hold a long-term position that you want to be protected, you have to be very careful. Do not allow yourself to be carefree because a huge amount of your money is at stake. Do not be tempted to give in to a burst of emotions just because the implied volatility is high. You have to evaluate the strike prices and months of expiration.

If the implied volatility is high and suddenly it drops, an implied volatility crash occurs. This occurrence is event-driven and basically a response to news such as product launches, earnings reports, and a major change in leadership of a company.

When such an event turns into a reality, it no longer remains an uncertainty. This diminishes the effects on the price of the options. However, since there isn't any guarantee in trading, you have to remember that the news may have caused a price move in the stock. Thus, selling high implied volatility options while hoping for an implied volatility crush is not a good strategy because the value of the option is not able to move. This is because of the movement of the stock price in spite of the implied volatility declining after the news happened.

Take note that implied volatility can vary in certain ways, such as the following:

a. By time to expiration

It is a factor that occurs in real-time trading and affects the option values of various strike prices. Generally, a higher implied volatility in an expiration means that the stock might move by a higher percentage during this particular expiration compared to others.

b. By strike price

The at-the-money implied volatility is usually the lowest. The price of an option may be broken into two separate components: extrinsic and intrinsic value. The intrinsic value depends on the option moneyness, the difference between the current stock price and the strike price.

Nevertheless, implied volatility does not have anything to do with this value. So, the deeper the in-the-money option is, the lesser the impact of implied volatility on the overall option premium. This happens because the implied volatility is the main determining factor of time value, which determines the price of the option along with the intrinsic value.

With regard to short option strategies, the time-value can work in your favor since the deep-in-the-money options do not have a lot of time value. The selling options that have thirty to forty-five days to expire accelerate the time-value decay. This is what you call the sweet spot of the time-value decay since it combines the accelerating decay rate with how much time value is left and has not yet decayed. In addition, the time-value decay isn't a linear constant. So, the closer you approach the expiration, the quicker it would drop.

Paper Trading the Trading Strategy

You can develop your skills in trading further when you continue to seek and implement new strategies. Through paper trading, you can make progress without much risk. Then again, when you make use of paper trading, you have to make sure that you incorporate the trading costs associated with the position in order for you to obtain the best strategy profitability value.

The Pros and Cons of Trading on Paper

Options traders practice trading constantly. When you use paper trading on a regular basis, you will be able to improve your skills in record keeping, market response, and method of analysis.

Your goal should be to learn about new strategy mechanics as well as how to reduce losses. It is also less painful to watch long out-of-the-money options go down in value as the implied volatility goes down when it is on paper.

Even though paper trading is not really trading and it does not completely prepare you for the trading world, it is still helpful in the sense that it encourages you to address your situation before you shell out money. It lays down mental grooves that help your brain rewire quickly.

So, what are the advantages of paper trading?

Well, it gives you feedback through the profits and losses that you acquire. It lets you incorporate the costs of trade as well as determines issues that you may not have thought of. It also helps you avoid any account loss.

How about the disadvantages?

As for the disadvantages, paper trading doesn't prepare you emotionally for financial losses. It also doesn't help you understand trade execution. There aren't any assignments and it doesn't address possible margin problems.

Electronic Paper Trading

In this day and age, nearly everything is done digitally. So, you can also practice paper trading using spreadsheets and other electronic platforms. According to scientific studies, you can maximize the rewiring of your brain if you write on paper. So, even though nearly everything, including paper trading, is done digitally, it is still more beneficial to do paper trading the old-fashioned way.

A lot of financial websites let traders enter various positions in a portfolio tracker that makes updates by the end of the day. Sadly, not every tracker accepts option symbols. Basic trackers can give position details that include price changes with losses and profits. More advanced platforms may include risk chart displays as well as other tools for managing a trade.

Trading Systems

Trading systems are methods that have certain rules for exit and entry. So, even though you use systematic approaches to strategies, trading systems are still more rigidly defined.

Keep in mind that in terms of system usage, you have to do these:

a. Create a position for every buy signal that is generated by the rules.
b. Exit every position once an exit signal gets generated.

Make it a habit to do the above-given procedures. Once you get used to them, you will be able to trade more frequently, especially when the market is volatile. See to it that you also consider your time commitments as well as any other potential changes. Incorporate all these factors into your everyday routine.

Of course, you must also know what you are getting. Trading systems are actually mechanical. So, there isn't any decision-making when it comes to system implementation. This is especially after they have been tested and designed. You do not think of accepting entry or exit signals. You have to stop the system completely if the system produces losses frequently or if something seems awry.

Formal systems are good in the sense that they minimize trading emotions and they allow for backtesting in order to have a sense of expected performance. When you begin to use discretion or when you decide to take on a specific trade, you will no longer be able to enjoy these benefits.

Your emotions will surface and you might give in to them. This would, then, affect the results of your trading. Hence, just like with any other trading strategy, you need to work with a system that suits your trading style as well as the size of your account. It should also be able to produce the results that you desire.

It is also true that the system rules are rigid and that it is common to build in flexibility. Filters can be added. They can serve as additional rules for trade exit or entry. Indicators can also be used since they serve as system parameters.

You can say that a trading system is good if it has the following characteristics:

a. Profitability across various markets, market conditions, and securities
b. Ability to outperform buy and sell methods
c. Ability to diversify trading tools
d. Suits your time availability and style
e. Stability with drawdowns that are manageable

You must be very careful when setting up a system and leaving it to go on autopilot. You must monitor the trades at all times. Likewise, you must make the necessary adjustments based on system performance reviews.

Doing a Backtest

Backtests rely on past data to identify whether systems generate stable profits or not. You can do a complete backtest by downloading data or mechanically tracking trades. However, if you really want an effective way to do it, you should use a software application specially made for backtesting. Just make sure that you actually test what you think you test.

When doing system backtests, you have to include the time periods that are long enough to capture bearish, sideways, and bullish markets so that you can acquire results from worst-case scenarios. This would allow you to experience realistic drawdowns. Drawdowns refer to the cumulative account losses that stem from losing trades consecutively. Nevertheless, you can always manage your risks by evaluating drawdowns.

Robust trading systems work well in various markets, including commodities and stocks among others. They also work well under various conditions, including bullish and bearish markets. See to it that you backtest the system in every individual environment prior to using it.

Also, when you review backtest results, you should look for stability and profitability. Stability actually refers to result consistency. As a trader, you have to know if your trades are spread over different trades or if they generate profits.

Take note that stable systems have average system profits that are close to median system profits. Their average profits also exceed the average losses of losing trades. They are able to sustain manageable drawdowns and they do not depend on certain trades for profit.

Systems also do not need to have more winning trades as compared to losing trades. A lot of trending systems depend on allowing profits to run for a smaller number of trades as losses are quickly cut on losing trades. In other words, you have to look for consistency. Do not allow yourself to be fooled into believing that you have a good system when you actually do not. You may get lucky at times, but this does not mean that your system is good.

If you want to design a good system, you have to consider the common characteristics of your best trades. Once you are able to create a system that performs well in backtests, you can move on to forward testing and run the rules in a shorter timeframe. In general, you can begin the test at the latest date of backtesting and then run it sometime before you implement it.

During the forward testing process, you can expect your returns to diminish. System trading is actually not the solution to profitability. It is simply a way that you can use to reduce the harmful trading emotions that you may have. It can help you achieve results that are more consistent.

How to Backtest Systems

In order to successfully backtest a system, you have to follow these steps:

1. Determine your basis of strategy. For instance, you may choose to capture conditions that are currently trending.
2. Determine your rules for entering and exiting a trade.
3. Determine period and market traded backtests.
4. Determine account assumptions.
5. Test your system and assess the results.
6. Determine any reasonable filters in order to reduce your odds of losing trades.
7. Add a filter depending on what you got for Step #6. Test the system and then assess the results.
8. Include a component that can help manage risks.
9. Test your system and assess the results.

Furthermore, if you want to determine whether a system is suitable or not, you have to evaluate the average value of losing trades and the consecutive and maximum losses.

System Result Review

When reviewing or designing systems, it is much more ideal to work backward. This way, you can manage risks more effectively. Evaluating systems that do not have any stops may appear to be counter-intuitive.

If you think about it, such stop levels are quite arbitrary. Whatever position you enter, the market will not care. You have to let the system determine viable stop-loss points during the backtesting process and then make up your mind if you think it is a good risk.

In the first run, the system results can seem favorable. Hence, filters are no longer necessary. The Max Adverse Excursion percentage was reevaluated to identify if the stop level is reasonable and may be added. If the results do not prove to be highly favorable, a stop loss will be incorporated.

For an indicator, different calculations may be used by charting packages. When you change systems, however, see to it that you compare the indicator values that give off the signals. This way, you will be trading the same system tested. You should always try to retest the system on a new platform.

Backtesting with Risk Management

Every trade approach has to consider risk management. You have to focus on the biggest adverse moves for strategies whenever you attempt to determine stops that allow for strategies to function correctly. You may implement the system or strategy if including this stop would maintain the stability and profitability of the system as well as if it remains consistent with risk tolerance.

About Cutting Losses and Taking Profits

It is possible to use a systematic yet not mechanical approach and also backtest it. Then again, the method you use in doing this backtest does not really matter. You have to watch for the major moves that happen on the generated trades. This would let you determine systematic and reasonable filters as well as help you minimize your losses.

Take note that stop-loss orders may lead to bigger percentage losses if the trade gets executed. Worst-case scenarios may happen if signals are generated at the close of trading one day while the security has a price gap at the open the following day.

Once you get used to trading, it would be easy for you to identify stop-loss points that manage risks. Nevertheless, you may still think about what if you had a trade that started moving the other way? It may have started to move when you realized that you do not have a good exit plan for gaining profits.

At times, traders tend to focus too much on the risks that they forget to determine good price targets. You have to be very careful with your moves. There are also traders who determine profitable exit points yet the conditions begin to deteriorate even before they reach the price level.

If this happens to you, what can you do to protect yourself? Well, you have to determine the stop–loss level. You also have to determine a trailing stop percentage or a dollar amount in order to reduce the amount of profitable trades that result in losses.

Such trailing stop has to be incorporated into the strategy or system that you use. You also have to test it. If you wish your system to produce the trailing amount, you have to assess the trades with huge favorable moves that yielded way less in the way of profits. Once you are done with your review, you can do the following:

a. Add a filter that can accelerate your exit.
b. Generate a trailing percentage with the use of favorable excursion percentage data.

Allowing Profits to Run

Effective trading strategies do not always need to have fewer losing trades than winning trades. All it needs is to outpace declines with profits. This is actually what happens with a lot of trend-oriented systems. Even if you get more losing trades, the average loss value is still much smaller than the average gaining trade value. Just as expert traders would say, see to it that you cut your losses as you allow profits to run.

When you sort trades by the greatest loss to the greatest profit, you will be able to review their statistics more easily. Even if you have to determine a strategy for gaining profits, you should also avoid cutting your levels of profits in a way that they do not outpace your losses anymore.

If you want to trade successfully, you have to have some pre-work. Make sure that you focus on these three things: cutting losses, preventing profits from becoming losses, and allowing profits to run.

When you trade options, you can set a dollar or percentage gain for a target area wherein you would take profits. You can benefit from this the most if you own more than a single contract. If every contract reaches the target gain, then you may be able to sell more than one contract while letting the others ride.

Being Simply Knowledgeable to Mastering Trading

Mastering trading strategies does not mean that you have to gain a profit from every strategy you use. It simply means that you are able to trade at appropriate conditions. It means that you are able to put the odds in your favor so that you can have a profitable trade.

Correctly managing positions is another component that shows discipline. You have to know when to exit a trade once the conditions change. This may sound easy, but it is actually not. You have to spend years of learning and training to become a master trader. Your goal should not be limited to simply knowing how to trade. Instead, your goal should be to become a master trader. You have to adjust your system constantly based on your past successes and mistakes.

Take note that the best trades are actually the ones that take the longest to find. When you evaluate individual and market stocks, you have to search for the proper set of conditions or setup.

This is more important than just finding the right trade. So, you may have to spend a few hours or even a few days trying to search for the right opportunity. Just like every other profession, trading may be described as one that is made up of minutes of sheer pleasure or panic combined with hours of boredom.

If you focus on the basic mechanics and concepts, you will be able to come up with a good foundation that lets you grasp advanced techniques quickly. You will be able to apply new strategies through paper trading so that you can avoid expensive mistakes.

Once you are prepared to take this new strategy live, you may reduce the costs of mistakes further by remembering to gain profits and reducing position sizes. Such a strategy keeps you in the market longer, letting you develop and search for strategies that would suit your needs and preferences.

Setting the Correct Pace

Beginner traders are often advised by more experienced traders to start out with paper trading. If you have just started options trading, you can gain more knowledge and experience by using straightforward strategies with paper trading such as purchasing calls and puts before transitioning to live trading.

Then again, there is no guarantee that the conditions of the market would be conducive to this strategy. Hence, you may prolong paper-trading for a few more days until you are ready to use another strategy or until the market changes. Always keep in mind that you have to focus on the strategies that seem sensible to you. This would enable you to develop mastery ultimately.

Beginning with Certain Strategies

If learning new methods and strategies is something that you like, then you will surely find a lot of opportunities in the financial market. Then again, you have to bear in mind that not every strategy works well in every market condition.

Even more, not every strategy will fit your risk tolerance and style. If you are a beginner, you are better off sticking to just one or two basic strategies to have a very good understanding of the premium mechanics and changes.

Different strategies are available and you can choose the ones that would let you earn a profit. Just like the methods of analysis that you prefer, you will realize that you have a list of preferred strategies as well.

More experienced option traders are advised to determine the current conditions of the market before exploring them. This way, they can arm themselves with the right information. You can begin with paper trading and then move from there.

In case you are fond of a certain strategy but you do not find the conditions to be right, it is recommended that you simply paper trade it. After all, it is much better to concentrate on the approaches that seem sensible to you.

Adapting to the Changes of Market Conditions

Traders cannot expect the market to be the same every single day. The financial market is constantly changing. Even if there is a continuous cycle of bearish and bullish phases, the financial market never stays the same. This is why you have to adapt your strategies to the changes in the conditions of the market.

You have to perform a strategy checkup when things do not seem to follow the norm. If the strategies that tend to work well for you begin to take a step back, then you have to do some thinking over the weekend. Perform a comprehensive assessment of the market. You may be able to detect signs of change in the conditions of the market early on.

Options trading lets you use strategies that may be profitable regardless of the conditions of the financial market.

For example, a bullish market with low volatility involves married puts and basic long calls. You can buy an at-the-money call option, an out-of-the-money married put, and an at-the-money call debit spread.

A bullish market with high volatility involves credit spreads and covered calls. You can buy an at-the-money call option, an out-of-the-money married put, and an at-the-money call debit spread.

A bearish market with low volatility involves debit spreads and basic long put. You can buy an at-the-money put option, an out-of-the-money put calendar spread, and an at-the-money put debit spread. A bearish market with high volatility involves credit spreads. You can sell an at-the-money-call credit spread and an out-of-the-money naked call.

A range-bound market can have high volatility. It involves a condor and a butterfly. You can sell two short options that are of the same kind together with a long higher strike price option and a long lower strike price option. A range-bound market can also have low volatility. You can trade at the money calendar spreads and at the money diagonal spreads.

You can have great options with the combination of options with options and stock with options. However, you have to remember that every approach requires mastery. You cannot just wing it. You have to actually know what you are doing.

You have to be thorough when you check out strategies. See to it that you also consider the circumstances of the present market as well as the kind of security that you used in your chosen strategy prior to discarding it just because it did not work the way you wanted it to.

It is highly possible that you will not be able to use all the available trading strategies. A lot of traders use different approaches along the way before mastering some of them. Your financial goal is the largest influence on the strategy that you choose. There are strategies that are more suitable for income while others are much better for capital gains. There are also those that hedge the risk of ETF portfolios and stocks.

When you gain experience from trying various approaches, you are able to maximize your profits using the strategies that you prefer. You are able to determine when you should hold your options, for example. Likewise, you are able to minimize your losses. For instance, you are able to tell when you have to fold.

Deciding on the options strategies you have to use is similar to market analysis. There are many different ways on how you can approach it. However, none of these ways would represent the single correct way. You have to go with the one that ultimately makes the most sense. Use your instinct. This way, you will be able to stick with your plan confidently in case the conditions change and you find yourself in hot waters.

Using Longevity to Achieve Mastery

Longevity is actually about having patience as well as staying power. It is about showing up for work every single day, no matter how hard things seem to be. Then again, in order for you to be able to do this, you need to stay on top of everything. You need to create a routine that you can consistently follow. It has to allow for the inevitable changes in market trends and volatility.

Take note that the bull market may run for many years. Volatility conditions may stay stable. Nevertheless, things may change instantly. In order to prevent heartburn and burnout, you have to be able to incur added losses in the event of market transitions as well as whenever new strategies are implemented. You will be able to achieve longevity when you are able to manage risks through strategies that yield unlimited gains and limited losses.

With paper trading, you can use techniques that would minimize your learning curve losses. Then again, there is another method you can use that can also have positive results. This method is known as proper position sizing. It is about starting out with a small initial position so that you can manage your losses. It also includes rules that would help you gain profits.

Of course, just like any other venture, trading is not a guarantee of success. You can never be too sure of the outcome. You need to work hard in order to increase your chances of winning. There is no such thing as an overnight success. Every successful person knows that. You have to spend enough time observing the different conditions of the market, having different emotions, developing trading skills, and making low-cost mistakes.

Identifying the Appropriate Trade Sizes

You can find a variety of techniques for identifying the proper trade sizes. They will help you identify the maximum dollar amount that is allocated for every trade as well as identify the maximum percentage amount that is allocated for every trade.

As the size of your account changes, the maximum percentage amount that is allocated for every trade changes as well. Conversely, there are certain markets that are best traded using the first approach. You have to determine how much money is allocated for every trade to increase your chances of earning a profit.

See to it that you always have a variety of options. This is especially true whenever you experience difficulty with the strategies that you use. Since options represent leveraged options, there is no need for you to allocate the same amount of money to the options position as you do for the stocks. Actually, it may not be a good idea to do this at all.

You can use your stock allocation plan as your base. You can assume an initial allocation amount by determining an options position that has control over the same amount of stock. See to it that you test and review your starting point.

You must establish your trade allocation amounts before you even analyze a particular trade. You have to know the maximum amount that is available for trading beforehand. This way, you can minimize the account risk.

After doing paper trading, you will use a new strategy. Make sure that you reduce the trade sizes further so that you can reduce your mistakes as well. Keep in mind that your main goal is to earn a profit in the financial markets, not to impress anyone with your trade sizes.

The more you develop your skills, the more you have to increase your position sizes to the tested allocations. This way, you can improve your gains. After all, the costs of options trading tend to be higher than the costs of trading stocks based on a percentage standpoint.

If you have prepared adequately and you continue to apply risk management in your trading, you will be able to increase your position sizes effectively. You will be able to realize the economies of scale with the costs of trading and your results will improve.

Taking Profits

As you may have already learned by now, one of the keys to succeeding at options trading is learning how to manage risk. Then again, you should also focus on taking profits. It is not enough to just have high numbers of profitable trades, you also have to gain a profit. In fact, your profits should exceed the trading costs, your losses, and conservative investment approaches.

You need to create a plan that involves reviewing trade results and strategies in order to benefit greatly. You will be able to reduce the number of profitable trades that become losses as well as let the profits run. You can say that you have evolved as a trader once you finally developed these skills.

Chapter 8: Creating a Trading Plan

Trading options can be regarded as a unique situation that needs a specific language and management style. Regardless of what you trade, you need to know how to run your business properly. You need to understand the costs that are associated with your business so that you can stick to your budget.

At first, some costs may be lower while others may be higher. You may even be likely to pay more for your learning curve and education. Nevertheless, as you go on with trading, you will notice these costs going down while your subscriptions to data services and analysis platforms are going up.

You should always remember that operating expenses involve losses. So, your goal should be to manage and minimize your risks. You can do this by identifying proper trade allocation amounts as well as the maximum loss for every trade. In addition, even though executing trades effectively is another step that you can take towards reducing your losses, you should still make sure that you come up with a good trading plan.

Having a Good Trading Plan

As you know, having a good trading plan is one of the keys to trading success. However, before you execute such a plan, you have to take certain steps into consideration.

For starters, the actual development of this plan is vital. You need to have a good picture of your goals. It is not enough to have a vague understanding of what you want to accomplish. You need to have all the details.

Nevertheless, development can be as basic as guiding statements such as "I would like to earn a lot of money" or "I want to have a consistent source of income". Once you get this big picture, you will be able to have more details.

A good strategy is to design a trading plan and have it revolve around just one purpose. This way, you can think that if you accomplish this goal, you are successful. Otherwise, you can think that your expectations may have been lofty. You may also think that your trading is not really compatible with your goals.

You have to have a quantifiable and reliable way to measure your failure and success beyond traditional methods such as annual percentage losses or gains.

The following are some of the guidelines that may be able to help you out:

a. Write down your proposed trading plan.

   Simply thinking or talking about your proposed trading plan is not enough. Just doing this can make you easily forget details. It can even make you forget about trading and important schedules.

   So, you have to write down your plans on paper or type them out on your computer. The important thing is that you are able to see them. This would encourage you to do better with your trading since it would remind you of your purpose.

b. Set goals that are realistic. Having goals is good, but make sure that your goals are something that you can actually accomplish. For instance, if your account is small, you have to refrain from setting goals that are too high. This way, you will not be pressured or overwhelmed.

   In addition, it is wise to break one big goal into several smaller goals. This way, you can accomplish every goal in a reasonable timeframe. You will not feel overwhelmed because the goal is small enough for you to achieve easily.

c. Use your goals as your measuring stick. Although meeting your goals is a good thing, you should not obsess about it. Remember that there will be days when you will not be able to reach your target goal. Nevertheless, you should not be disheartened because this can still be regarded as a good thing.

For example, if you are still able to gain a profit even if you do not reach your target objective, you can still say that you are on the right track. After all, you were able to gain something positive out of the trade. So, you have to search for ways on how you can improve your strategy. Just refrain from making so many changes without giving yourself a chance to prove whether you are right or wrong.

d. Keep records of your trades, expenses, and results. The results and trades will guide you as your plan evolves. The expenses will prove to be handy when the time comes for you to pay your taxes. In fact, you may use some of your losses and expenses to reduce your taxes. Having these records will allow you to manage your finances better.

e. Allow your goals and your plan to evolve. As time passes by, you may or may not become an expert trader who earns huge profits. If you are diligent and fortunate enough, you may make a lot of money from this venture. If this happens, you have to consider going full-time. Otherwise, you should still consider allotting more time for trading.

Managing Expenses

With trading, there are various costs that you have to consider. Some of them may be higher at the beginning of your career as an options trader and may even continue for the years to come.

You have to consider trading as a business. See to it that you manage your expenses wisely so that you can reduce them as well as their effects on the amount of money that you can earn when your business goes into maturity.

The following are the expense categories that you have to take note of since you will continue to encounter them throughout your career in options trading:

a. Education

The expenses associated with education include courses, materials, and learning curve expenses for new strategies and markets. As time goes by, however, these costs would decrease yet they will continue as you remain current with the market conditions. You need to spend on periodicals and books, after all. You will also spend money when you continue to learn new strategies.

Your learning curve is actually among your biggest education costs. This would begin to decline, however, once you find out how to trade under the best conditions for every individual strategy as well as how to use options with the right liquidity. It would also decline when you learn how to develop skills in paper trading, enter orders effectively for the best exit, gain profits, and allocate the right amount to trading.

b. Cost of Analysis

The more your skills improve and your trading yields profits on a regular basis, the more costs you may incur with regard to analysis. You may also include analytical tools in your expenses.

A great way to begin is to talk to other traders who use these analytical tools. You should also find out which ones offer free trial versions that you can use for a spin. These costs represent among the few that can increase as time goes by. See to it that you merely subscribe to a limited amount of services. You should also get to know them better so that you can maximize their usage.

c. Trading Costs

Do not just account for the commission. You also have to account for the slippage, which refers to the cost associated with a market spread. It is basically the difference between the ask and the bid.

You can compute for the slippage and commission percentage for the various size option positions established at various price points. This would be an ideal exercise for you as a trader.

d. Taxes

You have to determine the kinds of trading that are completed in your various account types. You can defer these taxes if you use the limited options trading that is permitted in retirement accounts. The complete details regarding the kind of options trading permitted in retirement accounts can be acquired from the Internal Revenue Service or IRS.

Additionally, when you establish some option positions when you have a position in the underlying, you can trigger a tax event. See to it that you contact your account regarding the tax considerations related to options trading. In the long run, the cumulative costs have to outpace the buy and hold approach.

So, when you borrow from your broker by trading on margin, you have to add a monthly margin interest charge to the trading cost. Take note that short option positions tend to have margin requirements that are complicated. You have to consider if the option is naked or covered for such margin.

If you want to use the strategies that require a margin in the long run, you have to make sure that you contact your broker so that you can completely understand each and every one of the account requirements and calculations involved. Then, you have to add the costs to the expenses.

e. Losses

In every business, losses will be encountered. There is no single business owner or trader, for that matter, who has achieved massive success without experiencing failure at some point in their career. So, if you want to become a successful trader, you have to prepare yourself for losses.

In the beginning, your losses may tend to be higher. Nevertheless, you will see them go down with experience and time. If you develop a good trading plan and stick to it, you can significantly reduce your losses.

Trading Plan Guidelines

Speaking of following a good trading plan to significantly reduce losses, the following are some tips that you have to keep in mind in order for you to maximize your chances of earning a profit and minimizing your odds of suffering losses:

a. Determine your trading allocations.

It is crucial for you to determine both your maximum allocations and total trading assets for your different strategies and assets. ETF and stock trading generally require bigger allocations as compared to option positions. If you wish to include a maximum allocation amount for your new strategies based on the results of paper trading, you should break this down even further.

b. Calculate the size of a trade.

You should also know the guidelines of maximum position sizes before you enter any trade. When you are done setting these guidelines, you will be able to identify the maximum amount of contracts you may allocate to a position more easily. To finish it off, you have to divide the options price by the allocation amount below the maximum. Refrain from using the maximum allocation to make assumptions.

c. Identify the maximum acceptable loss on the trade.

You may define the maximum acceptable loss as a dollar percentage or value. Since a fixed dollar value may be significant with a small trade or if the trading asset decreases, you may find the previous option to be more preferable.

You also have to perform trade result analyses on a periodic basis so that you can identify if your losses stay at sustainable and reasonable levels. You should be able to see how much money gets left on your account as well as whether or not it is sensible to go on with your present method.

d. Focus on exit and entry rules.

Oftentimes, the option entries are driven by trending and volatility conditions. However, they may also be time-oriented in which the positions have been created before a particular scheduled event.

The option exits may also be time-driven, such as pre-expiration or post-event. They may also be triggered by a movement in the underlying security. These methods have to be focused on supporting risk management as well as the maximum allowable loss.

Using technical indicators to exit usually does not give you any price for use with the risk calculations. Of course, you should not forget to identify the maximum loss price. You have to consider setting up another brokerage account that you can allot for options trading along. This would make record-keeping much easier and simpler for you.

Optimizing the Execution of Orders

Trading options successfully means having proficiency with the execution of orders. There are various factors that you have to keep in mind with this.

You have to understand the rules of order placement that are unique to options trading. You have to know how the different order types work. You have to learn how to do combination orders for positions that are multi-legged. You have to gain skills as you use the underlying to determine option exits. You also have to recognize the role of your broker in the quality of execution.

Take note that a learning curve exists for performing options trading. However, these are usually mechanical steps that you can easily master with continuous practice. You may do paper trading to improve your skills. However, nothing will beat real time action. You have to experience trading in real time to really know how things work. The experience will enable you to devise strategies that work for you.

Furthermore, you have to know that the offer is actually the best price or the ask available from the sellers.

Learning About Option Orders

Stock is actually constrained by its float. Options are not like this. They are not limited to a specific number of contracts, which are created by the marketplace and have unique considerations when it comes to placing orders.

Options are created when a couple of traders open a trade or create a new position. This increases the open interest for such an option. The open interest decreases when the trader closes the positions that exist. Floats refer to the number of shares available for stock trading as well as the outstanding number of shares.

Open interest is not updated on a basis of trade by trade. It is more of an end-of-day reconciliation via the Options Clearing Corporation. This explains why the option orders get placed in a particular manner. The Options Clearing Corporation has to maintain a straight accounting. This means that you also have to communicate more information when you place your option orders.

The Fundamental Rules of Option Orders

Selling or buying options may be done at any order. Opting to go short or long on a contract depends on your account's option approval level as well as the strategy that you use. You cannot go out there developing short option positions with unlimited risks until your broker allows you to.

The current market refers to the asking price and current bid for a security. Since contracts are retired and created based on the demands of the market, you have to enter an order in a manner that supports this options markets' end-of-day reconciliation. You have to use a certain language.

Say, the new position that you create is an opening order or the existing position that you exist is a closing order.

Chapter 9: Options and Futures

As a trader, it is crucial for you to know all about options and futures. You already know that options contracts give investors a right, but not an obligation to purchase shares at a certain price at any period of time during the effectivity of the contract.

What about futures? What about futures contracts?

Well, futures contracts are practically the opposite of options contracts. They require the buyer to buy shares and they require the seller to sell them at a certain date in the future, unless the position of the holder gets closed prior to the date of expiration.

Options and futures are financial products that you can use to earn money as well as to hedge present investments. They will both allow you to purchase investments at a certain price by a certain date. However, the markets for these products are actually different in the way they work. They are also different in terms of the risks involved.

Options are based on the underlying security's value. Stocks are an example of an underlying security. Investors do not have to buy or sell assets if they do not want to. After all, they have a right but not an obligation to do so.

Options are also derivative forms of investments. They can be offers to sell or buy shares but they do not represent the actual ownership of underlying investments until there is a finalized agreement.

Buyers usually pay premiums for an options contract, which reflects a hundred shares of an underlying asset. In general, a premium represents the strike price of an asset, which is the rate to sell or buy it until the expiration date of the contract. Such data shows the day by which this contract has to be used.

Put options and call options are the only two types of options. Put options are offers to sell stocks at a particular price while call options are offers to purchase stocks at the strike price prior to the expiration of the agreement.

To help you understand call options better, let us take this example: say, there is an investor who opened a call option to purchase stock ABC at the strike price of $50 for the next three months. Currently, the stock trades at $49. When the stock goes up to $60, the call buyer may exercise his right to purchase this stock at $50. He can also sell the stock immediately for $60; thus, earning a profit of $10 for every share.

Alternatively, the options buyer may opt to just sell the call and take in the profit. After all, the call option costs $10 per share. In the event that the option trades below $50 during the expiration period of the contract, the option loses its value. The call buyer will then lose his upfront payment for this option, which is known as the premium.

On the other hand, if this investor owns a put option and you want to sell ABC at $100 but the price of ABC goes down to $80 prior to the date of expiration, you will earn $20 for every share minus the premium cost.

Then again, if the price of ABC goes above $100 during the period of expiration, the option loses its value and you lose the premium you paid upfront. The writer or the put buyer may close out the option position in order to lock in a loss or profit at any time prior to the expiration date.

The writer can buy the option while the buyer can sell the option. In addition, the put buyer can opt to exercise his right to sell it at the strike price.

Futures

As you have read earlier, futures contracts refer to the obligation to buy or sell assets at an agreed-upon price at a later date. They are real hedge investments. In fact, you can compare them to commodities such as oil and corn.

For example, a farmer might want to ask for a reasonable upfront payment for his crops in the event that the market price goes down before they can be delivered. Then again, the buyer may also want to ask for a reasonable upfront payment in case the prices go up by the time the crops get delivered.

To help you understand futures better, let us consider this example: say, there are two traders who agree to pay $50 for every bushel price on a certain corn futures contract. When the price of corn goes up to $55, the buyer can earn $5 for every barrel. On the other hand, the seller can lose out.

Then again, the futures market has greatly expanded beyond just corn and oil. At present, stock futures may be bought on an index or on individual stocks. Those who buy futures contracts are not obligated to pay upfront for the contract's full amount. Instead, they can pay an initial margin, which is merely a price percentage.

Futures were actually made for institutional buyers who wanted to buy crude oil barrels and sell them to refiners. They also wanted to buy corn and sell them to supermarket distributors. Once a price is established in advance, the two businesses are able to avoid huge price swings.

However, retail buyers sell and buy futures contracts as a bet on the underlying security's price direction. They hope to earn a profit from the changes in the price of futures. They do not wish to take possession of products.

In addition, aside from the above-mentioned differences, there are many other things that set futures and options apart. Also, investors have to be wary about the risks associated with both futures and options.

Options contracts come with a lot of risks since they are quite complex. Both put and call options typically have the same amount of risks. When investors buy stock options, the sole financial liability they have is the premium cost during the period at which the contract is bought.

Then again, when sellers open put options, they become exposed to the maximum liability of the underlying price of a stock. If buyers have a right to sell a stock at $50 per share because of a put option, the individual who started the contract has to agree to buy the stock for $50 per share, which is the contract's value if the stock goes down to $10.

The risk to the call option buyer is limited to the premium that is paid upfront. Such premium falls and rises all throughout the duration of the contract. It is based on various factors, such as the distance between the strike price and the price of the underlying security. It is also based on the time remaining on the contract. The premium gets paid to the investor who has opened the put option. He is referred to as the option writer.

Option writers are on the trade's other side. They have unlimited risks. Still using our previous example, if the stock rises to $100, an option writer will have no other choice but to purchase the shares at $100 per share. This way, he can sell them to a call buyer for $50 per share. The option writer will then lose $50 per share in return for a small premium.

The writer or the buyer of the option may close their position at any time by purchasing a call option. This takes them to a flat. The difference between the cost to purchase back the option and the premium received is the loss or the profit.

It is true that options come with a lot of risks. However, futures are actually much riskier for individual investors. The futures contracts have a maximum liability to the seller and the buyer. When the price of the underlying stock moves, anyone involved in the agreement can put more money into their trading account in order to fulfill their daily obligation.

The gains on a futures position is instantly marked to the market on a daily basis. This means that the change in the value of the positions, whether upward or downward, gets moved to the futures accounts of the individuals at the end of the day.

Futures Contracts versus Futures Options

The short answer is that it actually depends on your time horizon and risk profile.

Among the initial decisions, new commodity traders tend to face is having to choose between futures options or futures contracts. Then again, even expert commodity traders sometimes experience this dilemma. Which one is indeed the better choice for trading?

Options and contracts have their own advantages and disadvantages. As you go farther into your trading career, your instinct will be more developed. Hence, you will be able to use your present situation to your advantage. You will be able to tell which one is more suitable for the time being.

Of course, there are also traders who choose to focus on just one. You can also opt for this method. Just make sure that you completely understand the characteristics of both options and contracts.

Futures contracts are regarded as the smoothest means to trade commodities. Compared to options contracts, they are more liquid. They also move faster than options contracts since options tend to solely move in correlation to futures contract.

Futures contracts are more ideal for day trading. They have less slippage and they are easier to get in and out since they move quickly. A lot of traders prefer to use spread strategies, particularly in the grain markets. They find it easier to trade calendar spreads as well as spread various commodities.

A lot of new commodity traders begin with options contracts. For most people, the primary attraction with options is that it is not possible to lose more than the investment. It is very unlikely to have a negative balance since the risk involved is small.

Options trading can be regarded as a conservative approach, particularly if option spread strategies are used. Bear put spreads and bull call spreads may increase your chances of success if you purchase for a long-term trade and your spread's first leg is in the money.

On the other hand, futures options are said to be wasting assets. Options can lose value each day. Their decay increases as they come nearer their expiration date. You may find it frustrating to be in the direction of the trade. However, your options will still expire worthless since the market did not go far enough to offset time decay.

Well, this time decay can actually work for you or work against you, depending on the circumstances. For instance, it can be advantageous if you use an options selling strategy. There are traders who sell options just because a huge percentage of options expire worthlessly. There can be an unlimited amount of risks if you sell options. Nevertheless, the chances of winning on every trade are better compared to purchasing options.

There are also options traders who like the fact that options are not as fast-moving as futures contracts. It is possible for you to quickly get stopped out of futures trades with just a single wild swing. With options, your risks are limited. So, you may ride out most of the wild swings in futures prices. You may find options to be the safer bet as long as the financial market reaches your goal within the set timeframe.

Chapter 10: The Best Platforms for Options Trading

Compared to stock trades, options traders offer higher profit margins to online brokers. Because of this, the competition in attracting clients is fierce. Nonetheless, such a market atmosphere is good for traders. After all, healthy competition is key to product innovation.

In order for you to succeed in options trading, you need to learn the theoretical aspects as well as put your knowledge into practice. Aside from knowledge and skills, however, you also have to have the right equipment. The following are some of the best platforms for options trading that experts recommend. It is ideal for you to learn about each and every one of them so that you can choose accordingly.

E*TRADE

According to many expert traders, it is the best overall options trading platform. It features $0 trades, the Power E*TRADE platform, and two mobile applications, which are highly recommended to beginner traders. It is easy to use and has a straightforward commission structure.

a. Stock Trades

Every trade is a flat rate of $0. $25 is added for trades that are assisted by a broker. Another $0.005 is added per share to the regular commission rate if you will trade during pre-market and post-market hours. Moreover, $6.95 is added if you will buy OTCBB or Pink Sheet stocks as well as penny stocks. Limit orders can only be used for placing trades for stocks that are under $1 per share.

b. Options Trades

Each contract costs $0 to $0.65 and is reduced further to $0 to $0.50 when making at least thirty trades for every quarter.

c. Mutual Funds

Every mutual fund costs $19.99 per trade. Depending on the funds, additional fees may be applied.

E*TRADE does not require a fee for streaming quotes in real-time. However, it requires a minimum balance of $1,000 before streaming quotes can be enabled.

Tools and Platforms

It delivers and innovates the ease, speed, and tools necessary for traders to achieve success. It features a charting engine that is powered by Chart IQ, which is a great third-party HTML 5 chart provider.

The highlights of this platform include integrated Trading Central technical analysis, smooth zooming and panning, thirty-two drawing tools, and a hundred and fourteen optional technical indicators.

The Power E*TRADE has an amazing blend of tools, position management, and usability. Hence, it is perfect for active and casual options traders. In fact, Power E*TRADE is the top choice of new investors.

It also offers an excellent experience for futures trading. It allows for the running of multiple futures ladders all at once. The orders can also be fired off easily using the Quick Trade widget. Furthermore, it allows for managing positions with the utmost ease.

E*TRADE also ranks highly in terms of research. It gives daily investors everything they need to perform in-depth market analysis across bonds, mutual funds, stocks, and ETF's among others. With this being said, this platform trails in web design areas as well as in-house market commentaries.

With E*TRADE, you can benefit from consensus ratings from third-parties and charting websites. It also has an in-house staff. Then again, the quote and screening of this platform could do better. It also does not feature live broadcasting.

Nevertheless, E*TRADE ranks highly in terms of mobile trading. Its mobile apps are rich in features and easy to use, even for those who are not that tech-savvy. It is recommended for those who are into options, futures, and stock trading.

It focuses on portfolio management, market research, trading, quotes, and watch lists. Its watch lists are actually streaming and customizable. Its quotes include advanced and basic charts, news, price alerts, and even added research like third-party reports. It even offers Bloomberg TV as well as basic trade idea screeners for mutual funds, stocks, and ETF's.

Young traders are especially impressed with the modern layout and design of the Power E*TRADE Mobile. You can actually switch between the advanced multi-legged options trading and their various pre-defined strategies to futures trading and Bloomberg

TV. You can also use advanced tools such as Live Action to help you search for investment opportunities that have pre-defined options screeners.

Power E*TRADE also has ChartIQ, which can give you a unique charting experience. In addition, you can take advantage of the user-friendly indicators for panning, conducting high-level analysis, and zooming.

Furthermore, E*TRADE ranks highly in terms of investment offers, education, and banking. It has everything you may need, including a full-service brokerage. It also has a variety of investment vehicles, from options to stocks to bonds. It also offers financial planning services via its Capital Management. Then again, this platform does not offer forex trading and international trading.

If you visit its official website, you can find lots of educational content. Helpful topics on investing, including retirement and stock trading, are available. You can read articles and attend webinars to help you broaden your knowledge and skills.

TradeStation

This one has been renowned as the best desktop options platform. Casual traders can benefit from the web-based platform while active traders can benefit from its desktop platform. Both platforms have $0 stock and ETF trades.

According to experts, TradeStation has highly robust desktop platforms. It is among the best in terms of technological advancements. In fact, it is highly recommended for mobile trading, options trading, day trading, professional trading, and futures trading.

With this platform, you can take advantage of various commission structures. Its most popular pricing plans, TS Go and TS Select, offer $0 trades and are very easy to comprehend. It also does not incur any monthly charges as well as includes free market data.

TS Select is the most popular pricing structure of TradeStation. It requires a minimum deposit of $2,000. It also includes access to the three trading platforms. These are TradeStation desktop, TS Crypto, and Web Trading. The first is the flagship product of the company. The second is a platform solely dedicated to cryptocurrency trading, and the third is a browser-based platform that was made for traders who prefer simplicity.

TS Go, on the other hand, does not require any minimum deposit. It offers unlimited $0 stock as well as ETF trades along with futures trades for only $0.85 per contract and options trades for only $0.50 per contract. Then again, even though it will give you access to all the platforms, you will need to pay $10 for the trades you place.

Under TS Go and TS Select, penny stock trades cost $0 for the first ten thousand shares. After this, however, you will need to pay $0.005 for every share. If you wish to direct the order to a particular venue, you will have to pay an additional $0.005 for every share.

With TradeStation, you can choose from two commission structures: unbundled and per share. If you are an active military personnel, first responder, or veteran, you can register for the Salutes program and enjoy free stocks, options trades, and ETF's.

If you wish to invest in cryptocurrencies, such as Bitcoins, you can start with just 0.5% for every trade. The commission rate will drop once your account balance goes beyond $100,000. In addition, you will have the opportunity to earn interest when you hold specific cryptocurrencies.

The functionality in the desktop platform is filled with dept. The tools include Scanner for custom screening, Radar Screen for real-time streaming watch lists, Walk Forward Optimizer for advanced strategy testing, and Matrix for ladder trading. Its coding language also allows traders to code applications and upload them on the TradingApp Store.

As for the desktop charting, there are over forty years of historical data available for stock charts. In addition, more than two hundred studies or indicators are available. They can be adjusted or reworked to your preferences with the use of EasyLanguage.

Then again, you may be displeased with the minor flaws in charting. It is not possible to plot y-axis markets for corporate events like splits, earnings, and dividends. Automated technical analysis is also lacking.

You will find TradeStation Web Trading simple and easy to comprehend. You can use it to manage your active positions, watch lists, perform stock chart analysis, place trades, and open orders. Compared to other flagship platforms, its chart-trading functionality is superb.

If you are into options trading, the OptionStation Pro will prove to be handy. It is a built-in tool that is designed for robust analysis and streamlined trading. Some of the options tool functionalities include streaming real-time Greeks, advanced position analysis, and grouping current positions.

Conversely, if you are into futures trading, you will like the TradeStation desktop. It features advanced tools that you can use to trade equities as well as perform futures trading smoothly.

You can also use TradeStation to screen options and full stocks, backtest equity, and stream forex and futures data. However, you may not use it to do traditional research for stocks. It is also not ideal for fixed income or mutual fund research as well as ETF research.

In addition, the depth and range of research available are limited. The market research is a combination of video and written content for both fundamental and technical analysis. You can also use the mobile application, which is designed meticulously and offers functionality for professional and active traders.

With regard to charting, the charting on the TradeStation mobile is clean and robust. It is everything you could ever want if you are demanding with your trades. You will benefit from the after-hours visibility, date range flexibility, full chart type, optional indicators, and filled order visibility. You will also benefit from the drawing tools.

If you are into trading options on futures, you can also use the standalone application. It is called the FuturesPlus, which offers various advanced tools that you can use for price visualization, advanced contract analysis, risk management through the Greeks, custom and predefined strategy builders, and real-time sales.

With TradeStation, you can have access to a variety of trading products. You will have full access to ETF's, stocks, options, and futures trading, including direct market routing, IPO access, and advanced order types.

As for the disadvantages, there is no international trading available with this platform. Also, the dividend reinvestment plans are not provided and every order for mutual funds has to be phoned in.

With TradeStation, you can also take advantage of educational materials. These materials will help and guide you through the desktop platform. You can access help guides, videos, and private learning sessions.

TD Ameritrade

This platform is considered to be one of the best tools for options trading by many experienced traders. It delivers $0 trades, outstanding market research, great trading platforms, reliable customer service, and industry-leading education for novice traders.

You can use TD Ameritrade on both your desktop computer and mobile phone. The mobile app is handy and ideal for daily investors. The platform is actually recommended for every active trader. So, whether you are into day trading, futures trading, or options trading, you will surely like TD Ameritrade.

What's more, TD Ameritrade is known for its artificial intelligence and advanced technology. It can be accessed via Facebook, Apple Messages, Twitter, Alexa, Apple CarPlay, and Android Auto.

In October 2019, a pricing war ensued. Thus, TD Ameritrade brought down the cost of its stock trades from $6.95 to $0. The options trades were brought down to only $0.65 per contract. Then again, even though ETF and stock trades are at $0, penny stocks are still at $6.95.

TD Ameritrade's thinkorswim is regarded as a top trading tool and platform. It is a desktop-based tool that is preferred by day traders, futures traders, and options traders. It is actually a favorite amongst casual investors.

This trading tool is also highly advanced in that it is able to stream dozens of charts in real-time. It also features more than four hundred technical studies available, making it favorable to the pickiest traders. Even better, all studies are customizable via the proprietary coding language of thinkorswim.

With thinkorswim, you can use fake money for virtual trading, plot economic data, chart social sentiment, perform backtesting, replay historical markets, and perform advanced earnings or options analysis. You can also conduct and create real-time stock scans, workspace layouts, and share charts.

If you prefer to use your mobile device for trading, you can install the TD Ameritrade Mobile or the thinkorswim mobile. The previous is ideal for daily investors who like customizable dashboards. It is easy to navigate. It is also filled with features that will allow you to sync lists, receive price alerts, read the news, and place trades.

The latter is just as great. Upon logging in, it will take you to your watch lists. It actually mirrors its desktop counterpart. You can use the indicators for charting as well as access Trader TV.

In 2017, TD Ameritrade was regarded as the first-ever broker to integrate with Facebook Messenger. It was also amongst the first brokers that offered Alexa Skill. In 2018, it also integrated with Apple Business Chat. Eventually, in 2019, it integrated with Android Auto and Apple CarPlay. Indeed this platform is the best choice for traders who are into advanced technological innovations.

Charles Schwab

With over $6 trillion assets, it is a unique order type for options trading and is one of the most valuable tools you can have as a trader. Its highlights include outstanding stock research, vast trading tool selection, industry-leading financial planning services offers, and $0 trades.

Charles Schwab is a full-service brokerage with an amazing, varied offering of investments that will surely satisfy you. It even has an excellent phone service. In fact, it is a top choice for IRA accounts due to its excellent stock market research offering. It also has robust tools that are great for traders who are into options trading, stock trading, and day trading.

Both ETF and stock trades are $0 while options trades are $0.65 per contract at Charles Schwab, which also lists the price improvements received on eligible orders. This makes it highly recommended for anyone who appreciates order execution quality transparency.

As for the fractional shares, you can buy a minimum of $5 from any company. If you are into penny stock trading, you can buy stocks and OTCBB companies for less than $1 per share. Every transaction fee related to mutual funds is $49.95 per trade. Take note that unlike other brokers, this one merely charges for original purchases. It does not have additional charges for selling.

Aside from the website, you can also access two other platforms: the StreetSmart Edge, which is a desktop-based platform for active traders, and the StreetSmart Central, which is a web-based platform for futures traders. Even though each platform has its own lowlights and highlights, both of them certainly satisfy a lot of traders.

The StreetSmart Edge is the flagship of Charles Schwab. It can be downloaded to any trading platform. It offers most of the whistles and bells that day traders and options traders need in their trading career.

The Trade Source is great for casual traders who are in search of simple tools that feature clean charting and streaming quotes. Then again, even though this platform offers futures trading, you should only trade on the StreetSmart Central platform. You are not permitted to use the website or StreetSmart Edge if you want to place futures trades.

According to experts, Charles Schwab offers one of the best quality research. It has a terrific in-house and market commentary. Aside from traditional third-party ratings, it also offers proprietary equity ratings that make the research experience more valuable. You can find these ratings throughout your platform experience. Furthermore, you can use the new Beta Research to research stocks, mutual funds, and ETF's all at once.

Interactive Brokers

This one is ideal for professional options traders due to its institutional-grade desktop platform as well as very low margin rates. Then again, it is not only attractive to professional traders. It is also preferred by many casual investors due to its user-friendly web-based platform and $0 trades.

Interactive Brokers is actually well known for giving traders access to more than one hundred market centers all over the world. It also offers professional traders industry-leading commissions. New users are even offered special margin rates.

In addition, there are two main pricing plans you can choose from. These are the IBKR Lite, which is recommended for casual investors, and the IBKR Pro, which is ideal for professionals.

With the IBKR Lite, you will not incur any data fees or inactivity fees. All ETF and US stock trades are $0. The options trade also have the same pricing as IBKR Pro. The primary caveat to this pricing plan, however, is that its order executions are of lower quality. Just like other brokers at $0, it earns profits from the order flow.

A lot of experienced traders go for Interactive Brokers because of its Trader Workstation. This desktop-based platform supports all forms of trading. If you are a seasoned trader, you will surely like the Options Strategy Lab,

Algo trading, Risk Navigator, Volatility Lab, Strategy Builder, Portfolio Builder, and Market Scanner.

You can also benefit from the watch lists, which typically include equities, options contracts, forex, warrants, and futures among others. You will also benefit from the IBot, which uses artificial intelligence to respond to clients via voice or chat.

Then again, in spite of these amazing advantages, Interactive Brokers is not perfect. You may find pulling up stocks to trade a bit tricky because of the wide array of securities. You may also not like the fact that automated technical analysis tools like the Trading Central are only available as paid subscription add-ons.

If you prefer to use your mobile device for trading, you can perform charting on your phone with ease and convenience. There are seventy optional indicators available. Then again, stock and index comparisons are not available for the mobile version of Interactive Brokers. It is also not possible to deliver stock alerts via push notifications. You can only receive these alerts through your email.

As for banking, Interactive brokers offer bill pay, a debit card, and the option to earn interest on cash that you did not invest. It does not offer traditional banking services though.

How to Choose a Trading Platform

Trading platforms are tools that allow traders to buy and sell assets on the financial markets at any time of the day. Now that you have learned about the best platforms for options trading, you have to figure out which one you will use.

Ideally, you have to go for the one that makes trading simple and straightforward for you. This way, you can focus better on your strategies instead of getting distracted by the platform.

The interface should be user-friendly and easy to navigate. It is great if you are tech-savvy; you will find it easy to use almost any trading platform. However, if you are not that adept with gadgets and software programs, you should go for a trading platform that is simple and easy to understand.

Trading platforms with complex interfaces are not recommended for beginners. You may only waste hours trying to figure out buttons instead of focusing on your trades. You will get distracted and you might even lose money if you use the platform incorrectly.

Account minimums are another thing to consider when choosing a trading platform. Be wary of brokers that require a minimum investment. Furthermore, you have to consider the broker's fees as well as your trading needs and style.

You want a trading platform that gives you flexibility and convenience. Go for something that is reliable and simple enough to be used on a regular basis. In addition, it has to offer paper trading so that you can practice at first. After all, it is not wise to start trading in real-time using real money without any real trading experience.

Conclusion

Thank you again for downloading this book!

I hope this book was able to help you learn about options trading so that you can become a successful trader.

As you know, nothing good in life comes easy. You need to be diligent, smart, and dedicated to succeed. You need to possess the right knowledge and skills. You also need to have the right character for trading.

Through this book, I hope that I was able to give you an overview of everything you need to know about options trading. I hope that the examples are easy and practical enough for you to understand. I also hope that the lessons are complete yet brief enough for you to absorb with ease.

The next step is to apply what you have learned from this book.

Finally, if you enjoyed this book, please take the time to share your thoughts and post a review. It'd be greatly appreciated!

Thank you!